People Sharing Jesus

People Sharing Jesus

DARRELL W. ROBINSON

Publishers Since 1798

THOMAS NELSON PUBLISHERS

Nashville • Atlanta • London • Vancouver

Published in Nashville, Tennessee, by Thomas Nelson, Inc., and distributed in Canada by Lawson Falle, Lt., Cambridge, Ontario.

Library of Congress Cataloging-in-Publication Date

Robinson, Darrell W., 1935–
    People sharing Jesus / Darrell W. Robinson.
       p.   cm.
    ISBN 0-7852-7929-6 (pbk.)
    1. Witness bearing (Christianity) 2. Evangelistic work. 3. Robinson, Darrell W., 1935– . I. Title.
BV4520.R64 1995
248'.5—dc20   94–45172
                                               CIP

Printed in the United States of America

2 3 4 5 6 7 — 99 98 97 96

Dedication

People Sharing Jesus is dedicated to the glory of my Lord and Savior Jesus Christ and to those who will find it helpful in reaching the lost for Him. It is my prayer that God will use it to equip many Christians to share Jesus more effectively.

I am indebted to many who have influenced my life and contributed to my understanding of how to share Jesus. I am deeply grateful for my Christian family and their encouragement, prayers, and support. My parents, Woner and Lillie Robinson, led me to Jesus and encouraged me when I surrendered my life to God's call to preach at age seventeen.

My wife, Kathy, has ministered by my side for many years as we learned and applied the principles of *People Sharing Jesus* in our personal lives, our home, and our church. Kathy helped guide our four children—Duane, Lori, Robin, and Loren—to become consistent witnesses. She has given much encouragement and assistance in my organizing and writing these materials.

I am grateful for the assistance of friends Len and Beverly Chilton who have modeled *People Sharing Jesus* in their own lives and utilized it in their ministry to equip believers to share Jesus. Beverly edited and helped organize the extensive outline of the material. Thank you to Jean Smith, who spent many hours typing it. As my secretary, she learned to practice these principles and consistently leads people to Jesus. She led my travel agent to the Lord over the telephone while she was working on my schedule. The travel agent joined our church and grew in Jesus.

My heart overflows with gratitude for the people in the pastorates I have held for their willingness to implement the caring, Jesus-centered, person-centered witnessing approach of *People Sharing Jesus*. Particularly I am appreciative for my friends Dan and Tommie Sue Sampson, who lived out the principles in their lifestyle. In a brainstorming session, Dan and I together came up with the title for this book.

My special thanks to my secretary, Virginia Whitehead, for her editing and computer assistance; and to Thad Hamilton, Thomas Wright, and especially Jerry Pipes and Rick Nash for their excellent leadership in the publishing of this book.

Contents

Foreword

As we move ever closer to the year 2000 with the dream of sharing Jesus Christ with every person in America and around the world, the pressing need of our time is to transform the multitudes in our pews into a sensitive army of caring witnesses for Christ. Darrell Robinson, in his newest book, *People Sharing Jesus*, provides a practical tool to meet this need. He powerfully communicates that personal evangelism happens naturally out of the overflow of an intimate walk with God. Through *People Sharing Jesus* you will find the inspiration, knowledge, and confidence necessary to successfully share Jesus.

Darrell Robinson will help you to experience the abundant spirit-filled life; listen to others and share Jesus at the point of their need; work in partnership with the Holy Spirit in recognizing and taking advantage of everyday sharing opportunities; turn everyday sharing conversations into sharing opportunities without fear or manipulation; guide a conversation toward Jesus; and share the Good News in several creative ways, with a simple and easy-to-use approach if your are just getting started, and a wide range of options if you are a seasoned witness.

The dream of sharing the Gospel with everyone in the world by the year 2000 is challenging, but not impossible. Almost all of us as Christians live in the midst of hurting people who desperately need to know Jesus Christ as Lord and Savior. May God use *People Sharing Jesus* to encourage and equip Christians everywhere to share Jesus Christ in a loving, nonthreatening way where they live, work, and play, that all my have an opportunity to say yes to the claims of Christ.

—Billy Graham

Introduction

People Sharing Jesus is based on several realizations from Scripture that led me to a concern for consistent involvement in reaching people. Every person without Christ is lost. The only hope of salvation is in Him. Unbelievers need the ministry of caring Christians who can sensitively share Jesus with them at their point of need. As Christians, we are responsible for that ministry.

Relationships are very important in reaching unbelievers. Lost people need to be receptive to the person sharing Jesus as well as to the Gospel. The time required to build a meaningful relationship conducive to receptivity will vary from a few minutes to several months or even years. The work of the Holy Spirit in the unbeliever's life and the attitude of the Christian witness will make the difference.

The realization of the need for person-centered, Christ-centered witnessing grew out of my own experience of salvation and growth in sharing Jesus with people. As a young person who had little church involvement, my shyness made it difficult for me to come to Christ. No one had ever witnessed to me or asked me about my relationship with God. The subject of Christ and salvation was embarrassing to me, so I would never bring up the subject. Praying aloud was a thing I never did. After I went to bed at night, I would pray silently before I went to sleep. I had observed when I did go to church that the preacher prayed with people when they made a decision to accept Christ. I was uncomfortable with the thought of praying aloud with anyone, especially a preacher.

Another barrier I faced was the fear of making a public profession of faith, being baptized, and becoming involved in church. I always felt uncomfortable going to church. I had a deep feeling for God and a desire to be right with Him, but I never considered myself to be religious. It was all foreign to me. I could not pray aloud like the church people. I could not sing the songs, engage in the conversations about the Bible or spiritual things, or do anything religious. The thought of going to the front of the church and making a public decision and then getting baptized terrified me. Water did not get any more than knee deep in West Texas where I lived. With no opportunity to learn to swim until I was an older teenager, I was afraid for the pastor to dunk me under the water. Yet I desperately wanted to receive Jesus. In my agony of conviction by the Holy Spirit, realizing that I was lost and fearing death and hell, I would pray silently at night for God to forgive and save me. But I never had the assurance that He even heard my prayer.

I needed someone to share Jesus with me personally. I needed someone to guide me through the conversion experience. My parents realized my spiritual need. Our family had not been regular in church attendance, even though my mother and dad were Christians and had been actively involved in church in their earlier lives. They very tenderly guided me to pray silently and receive Christ. I consciously confessed my sins to Christ and received Him as my Savior and Lord.

With Jesus in my life I found the courage to publicly confess Him and be baptized. I had committed my life to Him! I was determined to obey Him in spite of my fears.

Just out of high school, I married my high school sweetheart. We had both committed our lives to Christ and to His ministry. We enrolled in college together. Our son was born while we were in college. During her pregnancy, complications revealed that my wife, Betty, had a terminal illness. We struggled with her deteriorating health through our college years. Her condition required periodic blood transfusions and other medical treatment. I pastored a small church as a part-time student pastor. Both my wife and I worked at various jobs to get through college. Finally, Betty became so sick she could no longer work or go to class. During my senior year her condition deteriorated to the extent that I had to take her back to our hometown so our parents could help care for her. Baylor granted special permission for me to take my last three courses by correspondence. Betty almost died that spring! But God lifted her up and extended her life for another year. Through suffering and difficulty, God was teaching us how to live one day at a time, depending on Him.

Following graduation from Baylor University, my great desire was to pastor a church full-time. I was recommended to several. Some churches were interested. But when I would tell them about my wife's condition, I would not hear from them again. No church wanted a pastor with a dying wife. It hurt at the time, but we came to realize that God did not want us there any more than they wanted us. God has His special place for us. I preached one cold Sunday during a dust storm in a little ranch country church in our home area of West Texas. They had thirteen in Sunday School. The church appeared to be cold and dead. I told Betty that I wouldn't pastor there for anything. But I did! They were the only ones who would have me!

The pastor's salary was small. To supplement our income I took a job teaching school and coaching in the community. It soon became apparent that God had directed us to the place of His provision and of our effectiveness in ministry! God had put me out where the people were to minister to them personally and reach them for Christ.

As we developed relationships in the community through our work with the school, people began to come to church and to Christ. They loved and nurtured us as we gave ourselves to them. The church came alive and grew both spiritually and numerically. The church building filled every Sunday with worshippers. I learned that to reach people for Christ, it is important to go where they are, love them and minister to them, sharing Jesus at the point of their need. God had guided us to a place where He could sustain us and at the same time grow us and use us.

In spite of her illness, Betty continued to be active in witness and ministry to people and in devoted service to Jesus. The doctor advised us to allow her to be as active as she desired. He said that nothing she did would change her condition. She suffered intensely for months but continued in her radiant witness. Through her patient suffering, the door was opened for many to be touched for Jesus. We had been at the church sixteen months when the crisis came. I had gone to preach at a meeting fifty miles away. She insisted on going with me. We had to stop several times on the way due to her nausea. This was the beginning of the end. We entered her into a hospital a hundred miles away under the care of a kidney specialist.

During the ten days in the hospital, family and friends came, prayed for us and gave us support. Our church and other churches gave to help with the medical expense. Even strangers reached out to us with compassion. From her hospital room, Christians were ministered to and strengthened as they came to minister to her. Lost people were touched for Jesus.

As the end approached, my heart was filled with grief. A great heaviness settled in on me as I went to the hospital prayer chapel and fell on my knees to seek the face of God. I prayed for her healing, but somehow I could not leave it there. I had to add to my prayer the words of Jesus, "Nevertheless, not my will but your will be done." As I prayed, I asked the Father to heal her if He knew it would be best, but, if not, to please release her from her suffering and take her on home to heaven soon. As much as I wanted her to be healed, I came to realize that there is something better than physical healing. God has committed to give us His highest and best. His best is to develop us into persons who are like His Son. He works all things together for good for us, to conform us into the image of Christ (Rom. 8:28–29).

It was late Friday afternoon when I went back to her room. We talked briefly, then read the words of Jesus. "Don't be worried! Have faith in God and have faith in me. There are many rooms in my Father's house. I wouldn't tell you this, unless it was true. I am going there to prepare a place for each of you. After I have done this, I will come back and take you with me. Then we will be together" (John 14:1–3). We prayed together and embraced. She told me good-bye and closed her eyes, not to open them again. Early Monday morning she quietly drew her last breath and was absent from us but present with the Lord.

I drove the one hundred miles home with many thoughts and sorrows in my heart and mind. Yet I had a sense of joy and peace in realizing she was at home with the Father and would never be sick again. Our four-year-old son, Duane, met me at the car when I arrived at my parents' home. He asked, "Daddy, where is Mommy?"

I said, "Son, she is okay now. She has gone on to be with Jesus where she will not be sick anymore. She will not get to come back to be with us, but one day we will get to be with her in heaven."

Duane slipped down out of my arms with tears in his eyes as we walked together into the house. He seemed to understand immediately the depths of spiritual truth that many adults cannot seem to grasp.

Betty lived abundantly and died victoriously. Several people trusted Christ at her funeral. Through these days of difficulty, God taught me the priority of caring for people in their hurts and distresses. During the months of grief that followed, God sustained me through prayer, the promises of His Word, and the care of His people. I read a book during that time entitled *Try Giving Yourself Away* by David

Dunn. The thesis was that in trying to give yourself away, you never can. I learned that we grow through not focusing on our own problems but through giving ourselves. In the midst of life's deepest problems and burdens, people need Jesus. Sharing Jesus in caring ministry to people at the point of deepest need is a key to effective witness.

I came to realize that to love Jesus and to love people mean we will do our best to bring the two together. To reduce it to the simplest terms, loving Jesus and loving people is what Christianity and the church are all about. I came to understand that unless I genuinely care about the person with whom I am sharing, my witness will lack compassion and sincerity. Also, unless I study the Word of God, my witness will lack content. The caring witness sharing the message of the Word of God gives the balance needed to reach people.

A year after Betty's death, I entered seminary to continue my preparation for pastoral and evangelistic ministry. While in seminary I met and married Kathy, a lovely young woman from Mississippi. God had given me another ideal pastor's wife and a mother for my son. I was filled with happiness and gratitude.

Immediately after our marriage, while still in seminary, we helped start a new church. It grew rapidly until the attendance filled our building, and it became a strong church within two years.

Kathy had the heavy responsibility of being a pastor's wife and the mother of a school-aged son. During our first year of marriage she became pregnant and had a miscarriage. Through physical illness and mental and emotional stress, she became deeply depressed. I tried everything I knew to help her. Nothing seemed to make any difference. Neither she nor I could understand why she felt such despondency and why she could not pull out of it. In desperation, she entered a hospital for treatment. Her condition improved to the point that she could function, but the depression continued for several years until she was treated for a thyroid condition. Through sheer determination and strength that came by faith in her risen, victorious Lord, she continued her duties as a wife and mother and ministered to others in the name of Christ. She read extensively and prayed much. Eventually her depression was lifted through the ministry of the Holy Spirit, the Word of God, and good medical treatment.

During those years there were many times that I felt such an inner agony of helplessness that all I could do was to cry out, "God, help me! I trust you," then go on to do the simple things I knew He wanted me to do. In spite of the darkness of depression and the gloom it brings, Kathy and I knew the presence of the Lord by faith. We simply kept on by faith.

Kathy and I experienced the reality that a full and meaningful life in Christ does not exempt us from difficulty. In fact, we found that our greatest spiritual growth usually happens when we are going through our greatest struggles. Both Kathy and I grew in Christ through these trying experiences. I discovered that God works through every experience to grow us and give us His fullness. While He does not do these things to us, He uses them to develop and mature us into the persons we need to be. I found that one of the keys to a full and fruitful life is to focus on His purpose and reach out in ministry to others rather than focusing on myself and my own problems.

Kathy's time of depression was also a time of desperation for me. I determined to learn all I could about the illness and its related problems. I realized that in order to be of benefit to people I had to be able to understand and communicate with them. I had taken numerous psychology courses in college and seminary. But that was theoretical. Now, out of my own experience I felt the need to understand and communicate with people who have mental and emotional problems. I enrolled in the clinical pastoral counseling program at the Mental Health/Mental Retardation Center in our area. I spent time weekly counseling in the psychiatric units, as well as studying in the classroom.

In one case I counseled with a person diagnosed with catatonic schizophrenia. She had great difficulty in conversing on any level. I felt successful if she spoke a sentence during a thirty-minute session. I found that silence can be as effective in communicating with people as words in deeply reaching them at their point of need. I experienced the value of listening to what is said and not said, both in verbal and nonverbal communication, in sharing Jesus. From this setting I learned principles and techniques I began to use and to equip others to use in communicating the Gospel.

The truth dawned on me that many people need to be listened to as much as preached at. The balance of caring about the person and sharing the truth and promises of God's Word should guide us. This realization led me to a lifetime of study of how to effectively communicate the Gospel to people. In *People Sharing Jesus* I will share with you some principles I learned about sharing Jesus every day in life as well as participating in the church's planned outreach. It is my prayer that it will be used to equip multitudes of Christians to share Jesus with the lost. Equipping and involving all of God's people in sharing Jesus is the way to reach the multitudes today with His saving message, as was the strategy of Jesus in the first century.

People Sharing Jesus is *methodical* in its approach but is not a *method*. It deals with insights into the nature of people and what God has for them. In this book you will learn that You *Can* Live Abundantly, You *Can* Achieve Your Purpose, You *Can* Share Jesus with Confidence, and You *Can* Share Jesus in a Nonthreatening Way. Sharing Jesus begins with our own personal experience with our Lord. It is the natural outflow of the fullness of the indwelling of Jesus in us.

Section One

You Have Been Empowered to Share Jesus

He felt like a failure! Everything he attempted seemed to turn out wrong. He began to fantasize about being rich. He would do the one thing he could do to make the most money in the briefest period of time. He would take up the occupation of *bank robbing*.

The would-be bank robber began to plan his strategy. He sat up late at night working on detailed plans, drawing sketches and going over steps he would take in robbing the bank. But he could never seem to get around to robbing the bank. He would plan each night, but when morning came, his anxiety paralyzed him again.

One night he determined that his mind was made up. Regardless of his feelings he would force himself to rob the bank the next morning. The next morning an anxiety attack paralyzed him again. Finally he came through it and forced himself to get into his car and go to the bank.

The reluctant bank robber sat in the car in the parking lot from 10:00 A.M. to 1:00 P.M. trying to force himself out of the car. Finally, he got out of the car and went into the bank. At the teller's window he handed the teller his pistol. He stuck his brown paper bag in her face and said, *"Don't stick with me. This is a mess-up!"*

The prospect of witnessing produces a similar effect in

many Christians. Fear and self-consciousness create an imaginary barrier that all but paralyzes the believer. Then, when an attempt is made to share, it is with such tension that whatever is said may be quite unnatural.

Gayle, an outstanding church leader blurted out her frustration. "I cannot witness!" she said dejectedly. "But I will participate in the witness training seminar and go as a prayer partner if someone else will do the witnessing."

"That will be fine," responded the pastor. "We will trust God and see what He will do."

Her pastor had asked Gayle, as women's leader, to receive witness training, then to lead in witness training for women. With much fear and hesitation she came to the witnessing seminar classes. Through the Bible studies, the Holy Spirit had brought an unbelieving friend to her mind and developed a growing concern in Gayle's heart for her salvation. After much prayer that week, Gayle went to see her friend in spite of her fear and led her to Christ. She also led her friend's husband and son to Christ. The next Sunday all three of them confessed Christ and united with the church.

The woman who "could not witness" continues to share Jesus. She led her neighbor to Christ. She shared Jesus with her own son and eventually with her father. Both of them trusted and followed Christ. Gayle learned to effectively share Jesus and equip other women to do the same. She discovered the reality that God had equipped her with all that is essential to sharing Jesus and leading people to Him.

God has equipped every Christian with a unique personality and giftedness to share Jesus. Chapters 1 through 4 focus on how God has equipped His people for sharing. Every Christian can share because of what God has done and will do. He has provided for a life of freedom in Christ for every Christian. Effective sharing flows out of the indwelling presence and Lordship of Christ.

Christian witnessing is not about attempting to force ideologies and ideas on others. It is about caring people who have experienced God's love and grace carrying out the assignment of the Almighty God to share His message with others. Christians are on a mission for Christ to share the good news of what He has done to redeem all people and give them abundant and eternal life. Every Christian has been equipped to share about Jesus with the Word of God and a personal testimony of their own experience of salvation.

Authority for witness is not based on the world's approval. The world is often resistant to Christian witness. It is not unusual for non-Christians to attempt to intimidate Christians into silence about the One who set them free. The authority for witnessing is from above. We do not go because we have been sent for, but because our Sovereign Lord has sent us out (Matt. 28:18-20).

Confidence for witness is essential for us to be effective. The confidence of a Christian springs from his or her own relationship with God and from the understanding of what God uses to bring people to Himself. God uses a team of three to reach unbelievers for Christ. He uses the *Word of God*, the *work of the Holy Spirit*, and the *witness of the believer*. What confidence it gives to know that when we share the Word of God, the Holy Spirit will use it to draw people to Christ. Sharing Jesus and His Word is the greatest privilege one could have.

God has empowered each of us with the ability to communicate. We can communicate about Jesus. By listening, creating a rapport, and sharing in a nonthreatening way, any Christian can effectively witness. All of us do communicate. Commitment to communicate the Gospel of Christ is the key. Chapter 4 offers the help of a conversation guide for sharing Christ. It is designed to assist any Christian to share Jesus with others in a natural and nonthreatening way.

Experiencing the abundant life in Christ, realizing you are on mission for God to share Jesus, knowing how God works to reach people, and realizing you can naturally share Jesus will give you confidence to witness.

Chapter 1

You *Can* Live Abundantly

You are a *HYPER-NIKE*! What on earth does that mean?

Life had caved in on me! I was reaching up for bottom. My wife had died a few weeks earlier. I was alone raising our four-year-old son, working as a bivocational pastor in a small church while teaching school. Financially, I was struggling to pay hospital and funeral bills that accompanied a long period of deterioration before Betty's death.

That morning I was walking across the university campus reflecting on precious memories of my dear wife. I had come back to visit the campus where I had graduated the year before. I am sure there were tears in my eyes as I remembered the pleasant strolls we had taken in this very place not so long ago. I was thinking how quickly a life situation changes and how I would never feel the glow of her presence at my side again.

Questions about my future were heavily on my mind. "What am I to do? Should I come back to Baylor and prepare to teach in college? Should I go to seminary and continue to prepare for a pastoral or evangelistic ministry? Should I look toward the chaplaincy? I am a single parent! Will a church want me as their pastor?"

Suddenly I felt an arm around my shoulders. The voice said, "Son, how are you today?"

I looked up into the eyes of the tall man quietly walking beside me. He was one of my professors, Dr. Kyle Yates. He was one of the kindest, most gracious men I have ever known.

We talked for a while. He spoke comforting words and pointed me again to Romans 8:37: "No, in all these things we are more than conquerors through him who loved us" (NIV). Later, I remembered the textbook he had written and autographed. He had signed it, *Kyle M. Yates,* and below his name was the Greek word *hupernikomen,* then the Scripture reference Romans 8:37.

Back home in my office, I studied the verse. I discovered that the five English words "we are more than conquerors" translated one Greek word: *"Hyper-Nike!"*

Hyper means "more than, super, or far above." *Nike* means "a conqueror, a winner, a victor."

This wonderful word says that you and I through Jesus are far above any conqueror who ever won a victory. In recent years the word *nike* has been popularized as an athletic equipment brand name. The implication is *Nikes are winners!*

God was impressing my heart about the victory He had for me even in this situation. Through prayer, the study of God's Word, and several meaningful books, God showed me that life could never be the same for me, but that it did not have to be the same for me to experience His joy and victory. I realized that the One who gave me a meaningful life in the past is still on the throne. He is at work through all things to work out His purpose of making me like Jesus (Rom. 8:28). Therefore, because of Him, my life can be just as meaningful, or even more so, in the future.

Because of who He is in us and who we are in Him, we are *Hyper-Nikes.* I made the choice to claim the victory in Christ, to choose to be a winner, because of my position in Him who loves me.

"How long has it been since you have gone through one

day without experiencing victory in your life?" The question was asked of a Christian whose life radiated the presence of Jesus.

The answer? "About thirty years, I think!"

"That is fantastic! How have you been able to live like that?" the amazed questioner queried.

The mature Christian had a ready answer. "Some thirty years ago I made the wonderful discovery that Christ living in me in unbroken fellowship is the key to my living the abundant life. It is my own sin and disobedience that disrupts fellowship with Him and keeps me from enjoying His presence. So I consciously made the decision not to live one hour with sin in my life. I have sinned many times, of course. But every time I do, the Holy Spirit convicts me, and I immediately confess my sin and yield my life to Him in obedience. The fullness of Christ in my life and the unhindered flow of His love through me is my source of daily power and joy."

Successfully Sharing Jesus

God wants you and me to be successful in sharing Jesus Christ. The definition of successful sharing—sharing Jesus in the power of the Holy Spirit and leaving the results to God—is both exciting and liberating.

The definition has three parts: First, successful sharing is *sharing Jesus.* You may do any number of good things, even things that are necessary in building a witnessing relationship. You may live a consistent life, minister to people, and invite them to church. These and other positive actions are important. But this is only the beginning. *You have not really witnessed until you have shared Jesus.* Unbelievers will not experience the forgiveness of Christ until someone shares the life-changing Gospel with them.

Second, successful sharing is sharing Jesus *in the power of the Holy Spirit.* You can trust the Holy Spirit to do His work in drawing every unbeliever to Christ. The Holy Spirit fills the life that is yielded to Him. He uses the presentation of the Gospel, which is the power of God for salvation.

Third, successful sharing is *leaving the results to God.* If the person does not receive Christ immediately, the witness is still successful. If you sow the seed, you can trust God to continue working in the person's life, using your witness. We can leave the results of our sharing to God.

But before we can share Jesus, we must have a sense of His power and presence in our own lives. This abundant life—living moment by moment in intimate and unbroken fellowship with the Father—speaks louder than any words we might utter. On the other hand, a life of discouragement and defeat will destroy one's witness. Lost people will be attracted to Jesus if His representatives—you and I—radiate the love and power of our Lord. Therefore, the life we live plus the words we speak make up our witness.

The abundant life in Christ does not depend on circumstances, particular situations, or what other people say or do. It depends on our personal, unmarred fellowship with the Father. It is easy to drift into thinking that if we had more time, less stress on our job, or more encouragement and help from our family, friends, or church, we could experience daily victory. But we are jolted by the words of Paul in Philippians 4:4 to realize that God provides personal spiritual empowerment for us in every experience of life: "Rejoice in the Lord always. I will say it again: Rejoice!" (NIV). Paul penned these words in the solitude of a Roman prison cell. (Some have estimated that he spent fourteen of some twenty-eight years of ministry in prison.) Instead of anxiously pacing his cell, bemoaning his fate as Caesar's prisoner, he confidently wrote "as a prisoner of the Lord" (Eph. 4:1). And his letters shook the Roman Empire to its foundations.

Paul did not chafe at being the prisoner of Caesar, feeling

that Caesar was only an instrument and that his own imprisonment was by God's design. Paul was such an activist that he probably never would have been still long enough to write some of the epistles of the New Testament had he not been confined. But as a result of his faithfulness in the midst of trouble, his words have come to us across the centuries to encourage Christians and to win multitudes to Christ.

Six Keys to Abundant Living

God desires that each of His children live victoriously every moment of every day. The secret is a simple but powerful six-step process. The process does not require months, days, or even hours. The experience with God may, in fact, be sudden and instantaneous—the moment the heart of a believer is responsive to the Holy Spirit. The question is, "How can this happen in a life?"

Your Enemy Is Satan

Do not be deceived by the enemy nor ignorant of his strategies. The enemy attacks often and subtly. But who is our enemy?

God is not our enemy. He is on our side. He has committed to give us His highest and best. He is working out everything that happens to us for our good and to conform us to the image of Christ (Rom. 8:28–31). He has proven that He is for us by not sparing His Son. Through Him, God freely gives us His best (Rom. 8:32). God tempts no one to sin. Yet He permits us to be tested so that our weaknesses will surface and we can grow strong through overcoming the trial. Faith is strengthened by being put to the test (James 1:2–6, 12–15). He assures us that He will not allow us to be tested beyond our ability to endure and overcome, but promises to provide a way of escape (1 Cor. 10:13).

Then who is the enemy? The devil, Satan, is our enemy (2 Cor. 4:4; James 4:7; 1 Peter 5:8). His methods (wiles) are deceitful (Eph. 6:11–12). The devil is not omniscient, but he is smart. He knows our defects and points of vulnerability. He knows exactly at what points to appeal to us.

The devil uses a threefold strategy. He uses the ungodly world, its philosophies, and its appeals in his attack on Christians. "Our foolish pride comes from this world, and so do our selfish desires and our desire to have everything we see. None of this comes from the Father" (1 John 2:16).

First, Satan uses our own innate desires against us. The drives to satisfy the need for food, love, approval, sex, and achievement are God-given. But Satan appeals to us to satisfy these God-given desires in a God-forbidden way. The desire becomes lust only as we attempt to step outside God's plan. Then lust gives birth to sin. "But each one is tempted when, by his own evil desire, he is dragged away and enticed. Then, after desire has conceived, it gives birth to sin; and sin, when it is full-grown, gives birth to death" (James 1:14–15 NIV).

Second, Satan uses the appeal of the things we see. What the eye sees affects the mind. Imaginations of evil are planted in the mind through the lust of the eye.

In 1 Kings 21, King Ahab saw the flourishing vineyard belonging to his neighbor. He offered to buy the garden, but Naboth wanted to keep the property because he had inherited it from his father. The king sulked and brooded about the field he coveted but could not have. His wife plotted with him to kill Naboth and commandeer the vineyard. The Scripture says, "There was never a man like Ahab, who sold himself to do evil in the eyes of the LORD, urged on by Jezebel his wife" (1 Kings 21:25 NIV).

Even King David, the man after God's own heart, let his roving eye lead him astray when he watched Uriah's wife bathe from his rooftop.

Satan wants our eyes to steer our hearts. Such arguments from Satan attack the thought life of the Christian.

> For though we walk in the flesh, we do not war according to the flesh. For the weapons of our warfare are not carnal but mighty in God for pulling down strongholds, casting down arguments and every high thing that exalts itself against the knowledge of God, bringing every thought into captivity to the obedience of Christ. (2 Cor. 10:3–5 NKJV)

Through the window of the eye, lustful thoughts enter the mind. Lustful desires well up in the heart. Through them, Satan establishes fortresses in the lives of Christians. These are bases of operation and pockets of poison Satan uses to defeat us.

Third, he uses pride. Pride is at the root of every kind of sin (James 4:1–11). Through a spirit of pride, Christ is dethroned in a life. Satan wields powerful influence through the old self-life of the Christian. Pride leads the believer to think and plan independently of God. "For as he thinks in his heart, so is he" (Prov. 23:7 NKJV).

Realize that Satan will continue his campaign to destroy your victory in Christ. If he can do so, he will negate the influence of your life and render your witness powerless.

Your Battle Has Already Been Won

At the cross Jesus paid the sin debt once for all. The victory over sin has been won forever. Claim the fact that through His finished work—His death on the cross and His resurrection—sin has no more power over your life. Satan has already been defeated.

To live with unresolved feelings of guilt from past sins robs Christians of the inner confidence essential to effective sharing. Accepting what Jesus did in His work on the cross frees the conscience of the child of God through experiencing forgiveness. "But Christ was sinless, and he offered himself as an eternal and spiritual sacrifice to God. That's why his blood is much more powerful and makes our consciences clear. Now we can serve the living God and no longer do things that lead to death" (Heb. 9:14). Because Christ lives in you, you have the potential of victory in daily life over sin and Satan (Gal. 2:20).

Your Power Comes from the Father

Through the new-birth experience, God gives His child two "ships"—a relationship and a fellowship. The relationship is between Father and child. When you become a child of God, you belong to Him. He is your Father. And your body is His home. "Surely you know that your body is a temple where the Holy Spirit lives. The Spirit is in you and is a gift from God. You are no longer your own. God paid a great price for you. So use your body to honor God" (1 Cor. 6:19–20). As a newborn child of the Father who is indwelt by His Spirit, you then have intimate fellowship with Him.

Your relationship with the Father never changes, since the relationship depends upon the Father's faithfulness. God is faithful to keep that which has been committed to Him (2 Tim. 1:12). Once born again, a person will never cease to be a beloved child of the Father. You may be a disobedient child, but you will still be His child. The Father does not cast His children away. Instead, He will work in your life to give you the power to overcome. "God is working in you to make you willing to obey Him" (Phil 2:13).

Through His Word and through the leadership of the Holy Spirit, God guides His children in victory, fulfilling His purpose in their lives (Rom. 8:14). However, if a child persists in disobedience, God will discipline the child (Heb. 12:5–11). His discipline is not punitive, but corrective and redemptive. Discipline is His love in action to lead His child to repentance, cleansing, and abundance.

Unlike the *relationship* with the Father, which never changes, *fellowship* does change, since fellowship depends upon the child's faithfulness to the Father. When we are disobedient, we experience inner turmoil and may ultimately be led to spiritual defeat.

As a boy I never doubted my dad's love. Often, before leaving home on a business trip, he would give my brother and me assignments to complete while he was away. We always knew that when he came home, he would have a little bag of goodies for us. We would race to meet him when we saw him coming—that is, if we had done what he told us to do. If not, we avoided him. If I had failed to carry out his instructions, I dreaded seeing him. You see, he was still my dad, but my disobedience drove a wedge between us. The feeling of distance would continue until I admitted my disobedience, asked forgiveness, and did what he asked me to do.

Power in Christ depends upon maintaining an intimate fellowship with Him, unmarred by disobedience. "Jesus said to his disciples: If you love me, you will do as I command. . . . If you love me, you will do what I have said, and my Father will love you. I will also love you and show you what I am like" (John 14:15, 21).

Your Failure Isn't Final

When disobedience disrupts this sweet fellowship, all is

13

not lost. God will not desert us, but will provide a way back to Him.

At the time of the new birth, which is transacted by the Holy Spirit, the new Christian turns over the controls of his or her life to Christ and is filled with the Spirit. When the new believer sins, however, the Holy Spirit still indwells the life, but is no longer in control of it. He is *resident*, but not *president* of your life. He is a *passenger*, but not the *pilot*!

When sin comes into your life, the Holy Spirit is quenched, just as water poured on fire quenches the fire. "Do not put out the Spirit's fire" (1 Thess. 5:19 NIV). Sin in the life of a Christian grieves the Holy Spirit. "And do not grieve the Holy Spirit of God, with whom you were sealed for the day of redemption. Get rid of all bitterness, rage and anger, brawling and slander, along with every form of malice. Be kind and compassionate to one another, forgiving each other, just as in Christ God forgave you" (Eph. 4:30–32 NIV). When the Holy Spirit is grieved, He communicates grief, not joy, to your spirit. Living in a state of disobedience is a dismal, joyless existence for the Christian.

God has described this sad state for us in 1 John 1: "If we say that we have not sinned, we are fooling ourselves, and the truth is not in our hearts. . . . If we say that we have not sinned, we make God a liar and his message is not in our hearts" (vv. 8, 10). But He also tells us how our fellowship with Him may be restored: "If we confess our sins to God, he can always be trusted to forgive us and take our sins away" (v. 9).

Confess your sins! Confession is the act of agreeing with God about your sins. The word *confess* is a graphic word in the Greek language—*homologeo. Homo* means "the same as" or "alike." *Logos* means "a word," "to speak," "to say." Thus, *homologeo* means "to say the same word as" or "to agree" with God about your sin. Call sin what God calls it. Name it. Be specific.

Human nature recoils against confessing sin. It does not

want to confess. Instead, it tends to make excuses, to rationalize, to justify, to hide it or ignore it, to blame others, or to deny it. Yet God says to confess.

A salesman often padded his expense account. He became a Christian. Each night he read his Bible and prayed. He was growing, but one night he found it difficult to pray. The matter of his expense account kept interrupting his thoughts. He had added items to the expense account that did not belong there. Convicted, he began to pray about the matter.

"Oh, God, I have been padding my expense account. God, I have taken money that did not belong to me. I have stolen! I'm a thief! Forgive me! Cleanse me!"

The next day, when he was tempted to do it again, he could not. God had forgiven and cleansed him. God forgives when His children repentantly confess. To forgive means "to erase." The sin "disappears" like a cloud in the sky disperses before your eyes. God does not even remember it anymore. He puts it as far away as the east is from the west (Jer. 31:34; Ps. 103:12). He enables us to leave it behind (Phil. 3:13).

God not only forgives, He cleanses when the believer confesses sin. The Greek word for "cleanse," *katharidzo*, is the root of two English words. *Catheterize* is a medical term used to denote the removing of impurities from the physical body. *Catharsis* is a psychological term applied to the venting of pent-up emotions so that release and relief are achieved.

When God cleanses you spiritually, He removes the spiritual impurities from your inner life. Sin is foreign to the life of a Christian. It produces discomfort and pain. Pain is God's gift to call attention to the marred fellowship so the Christian will deal with sin through repentance and confession.

To illustrate, suppose a sliver of steel gets into your eye. Your entire body responds, reacting instinctively to the

15

danger. This harmful foreign object, which has the potential of inducing blindness, is painful. If there were no pain, the danger might be ignored. Involuntarily, your eye closes for protection. Your tear duct springs into action to wash it out. If that fails, your hand leaps to the rescue to wipe it away. Then your mouth acts to call for help. Your feet take you to get help. This is an emergency! The steel must be removed!

Sin is foreign and destructive to the Christian life. As long as the sin is present, pain and misery will also be present. God permits the pain sin brings so that you will confess and forsake the sin. Through the cleansing provided by the blood of Christ shed on the cross, He removes it from your life (1 John 1:7). How wonderful it is to know His forgiveness and cleansing.

Your Past Is Not a Prelude to the Future

Confess your sins to the Father and claim His forgiveness and cleansing. Then in prayer, by faith, ask God to fill you anew with the Holy Spirit. Claim the Holy Spirit's control in your life (Eph. 5:18). It is God's will for every Christian to be filled continually with His Spirit. It is not a matter of the emotion, though feeling is affected. It is a matter of faith. Simply trust Him and take Him at His word that He will fill you as you desire to be filled (John 6:37–39).

Obey Jesus (John 14:21). Go on to act as if the victory is yours. This is faith! The question comes, "What if I sin again?" Then confess it again. Don't wait until you are burdened down with a load of sin. Don't wait until Sunday when you are in church. Don't wait until night or the next day or some more convenient time. Confess it immediately, claim the fullness of the Holy Spirit, and obey Him. Practice moment-by-moment confession of sin. The time will come when you will realize that you have totally overcome the sin through the presence and power of the Holy Spirit.

From Texas history comes the story of the conversion of Sam Houston. At one time, the Texas hero was called "The Old Drunk." While he was governor of Tennessee, his wife left him. In despair he resigned as governor and tried to escape his problems by going to live among the Cherokee Indians. He stayed drunk much of the time. It is said that the Indians, as they walked through the forest, would have to move him out of the path where he lay in a stupor.

Later, he went to Texas, where he became the great hero of the Texas revolution when he routed General Santa Ana's Mexican army. Houston's battle cry, "Remember the Alamo!" helped win independence for Texas. He married the daughter of a Baptist preacher and later trusted Christ, but he still had some of his old tendencies. One day as he rode along a trail, his horse stumbled. Houston spontaneously cursed, reverting to his old habit. Immediately he was convicted of his sin. He got off his horse, knelt down on the trail, and cried out to God for forgiveness. Houston had already received Christ, but God was teaching him to live in fellowship with Him moment by moment. And as soon as the Holy Spirit made Sam Houston aware of his sin, he confessed it.

Your Key to Abundant Living Is Praise

Now, praise God in prayer. Thank Him for forgiving and cleansing you. Thank Him for filling you with His Holy Spirit.

Read Psalm 139:23–24: "Search me, O God, and know my heart; test me and know my anxious thoughts. / See if there is any offensive way in me, and lead me in the way everlasting" (NIV). And I know that, like me, the desire of your heart is for His Holy Spirit to make you sensitive to His direction. You want to commit yourself wholeheartedly to Him. You desire to be available for Him to use you for His glory. Ask Him to give you many opportunities to share Jesus with others. Experiencing the fullness of Jesus in your life will strengthen your witness and allow His power to flow through you.

Chapter One: Personal Review Questions

1. What is the definition of successful sharing?

2. In what ways can a person insure that he/she is walking in the Spirit? What is the danger if any of these six elements of maintaining moment-by-moment fellowship are missing?

3. While it is possible to experience broken fellowship with God, what keeps us from ever losing our relationship with Him as our Father? (If fellowship is broken with the Father, what does it take to restore that fellowship?)

4. Why is it necessary to pursue consistent fellowship with God in order to be prepared to share the Gospel with another person?

Chapter 2

You *Can* Achieve
Your Purpose

Be Sensitive to Unbelievers

Realizing that God has empowered every Christian to witness helps us focus on sharing Jesus with every person. They need to know that Jesus came to seek and to save the lost (Luke 19:10). If our hearts beat with the heart of our Master, they will beat for people who are separated from Him. God has given every Christian an experience with Jesus to share. He can and will use the life and words of every Christian to reach the unbeliever.

Unbelievers are *not* the enemy. We do not need to treat them as such. All kinds of behaviors are manifested by unbelievers. *People act like they act because they are where they are.* The lost act lost because they *are* lost. We are not to condemn, nor intimidate, nor avoid them.

Neither should we be intimidated by them.

Each of us is on assignment from our Lord to reach unbelievers. They are precious to Him. Our sensitivity to non-Christians' spiritual needs is a major factor that determines whether or not we will reach them. We must become consciously alert and involved in seeking out people with whom we can share Jesus. As individual Christians, we are responsible to God for our influence on unbelievers' lives.

New Christians who have confessed Christ as their Savior and Lord want to tell others about Him. Witnessing is a natural expression of our love and commitment to Him. Immediately following his experience with Jesus, Andrew did what anyone would do: he found his brother, Simon Peter, and brought him to Jesus (John 1:40–42).

Charles, a young engineer who worked at NASA, accepted Christ as his Savior. A couple of days later, in discipling him, the friend who had led Charles to the Lord told him that God wanted to use him as a witness. After the friend went on to define witnessing, Charles was delighted. "Oh, I've already been doing that! I went back to the lab after I invited Christ into my life and told everybody. I talked to them about Jesus and some of them are interested!" Having come to know Jesus, it was natural for Charles to share Him with his fellow workers so that they could know Him too.

When the new Christian's church places a strong emphasis on sharing Jesus, the fervor for witness will continue to grow. If not, the spark of desire to share Jesus will likely become dormant. If you have become discouraged about sharing Jesus, you can recover spiritual concern for the lost and encouragement in reaching them. As you pray and yield to the Holy Spirit, He will fan the spark into a holy fire for sharing Jesus with others.

As a fifth grader, I received a Gideon New Testament at school. Even though I had not yet received Christ, I began to read it. Matthew 4:19 captivated my attention: "'Follow me,' Jesus said, 'and I will make you fishers of men'" (NIV). It was clear to me even then: If I follow Jesus, I will be fishing for men. If I am not fishing, I am not following.

A disciple is a learner and a follower of Jesus. Jesus came and died that the lost may know Him. If we are learning of Him and following Him, then we will share the passion of Jesus for people to know Him.

The following is a convicting modern parable written by Pastor John M. Drescher:

A Plea for Fishing

Now it came to pass that a group existed who called themselves fishermen. And lo, there were many fish in the waters all around. In fact, the whole area was surrounded by streams and lakes filled with fish. And the fish were hungry.

Week after week, month after month, and year after year, these who called themselves fishermen met in meetings and talked about their call to fish, the abundance of fish, and how they might go about fishing. Year after year they carefully defined what fishing means, defended fishing as an occupation, and declared that fishing is always to be a primary task of fishermen.

Continually, they searched for new and better methods of fishing and for new and better definitions of fishing. Further they said, "The fishing industry exists by fishing as fire exists by burning." They loved slogans such as "Fishing is the task of every fisherman." They sponsored special meetings called "Fishermen's Campaigns" and "The Month for Fishermen to Fish." They sponsored costly nationwide and worldwide congresses to discuss fishing and to promote fishing and hear about all the ways of fishing such as the new fishing equipment, fish calls, and whether any new bait had been discovered.

These fishermen built large, beautiful buildings called "Fishing Headquarters." The plea was that everyone should be a fisherman and every fisherman should fish. One thing they didn't do, however: They didn't fish.

In addition to meeting regularly, they organized a board to send out fishermen to other places where there were many fish. The board hired staffs and appointed committees and held many meetings to define fishing, to defend fishing, and to decide what new streams should be thought about. But the staff and committee members did not fish.

Large, elaborate, and expensive training centers were built whose original and primary purpose was to teach fishermen how to fish. Over the years courses were offered on the needs of fish, the nature of fish, where to find fish, the psychological reactions of fish, and how to approach and feed fish. Those who taught had doctorates in fishology, but the teachers did not fish. They only taught fishing. Year after year, after tedious training, many were graduated and were given fishing licenses. They were sent to do full-time fishing, some to distant waters which were filled with fish.

Many who felt the call to be fishermen responded. They were commissioned and sent to fish. But like the fishermen back home, they never fished. Like the fishermen back home, they engaged in all kinds of other occupations. They built power plants to pump water for fish and tractors to plow new waterways. They made all kinds of equipment to travel here and there to look at fish hatcheries. Some also said that they wanted to be part of the fishing party, but they felt called to furnish fishing equipment. Others felt their job was to relate to the fish in a good way so the fish would know the difference between good and bad fishermen. Others felt that simply letting the fish know they were nice, land-loving neighbors and how loving and kind they were was enough.

After one stirring meeting on "The Necessity for Fishing," one young fellow left the meeting and went fishing. The next day he reported that he had caught two outstanding fish. He was honored for his excellent catch and scheduled to visit all the big meetings possible to tell how he did it. So he quit his fishing in order to have time to tell about the experience to the other fishermen. He was also placed on the Fishermen's General Board as a person having considerable experience.

Now it's true that many of the fishermen sacrificed and put up with all kinds of difficulties. Some lived near the water and bore the smell of dead fish every day. They received the ridicule of some who made fun of their fishermen's clubs and the fact that they claimed to be fishermen yet never fished. They wondered about those who felt it was of little use to attend the weekly meetings to talk about fishing. After all, were they not following the Master who said, "Follow me, and I will make you fishers of men"?

Imagine how hurt some were when one day a person suggested that those who don't catch fish were really not fishermen, no matter how much they claimed to be. Yet it did sound correct. Is a person a fisherman if, year after year, he never catches a fish? Is one following if he isn't fishing?

As the fishing parable implies, our human tendency is to move away from rather than toward, evangelism. It is easy to be diverted from actually sharing Jesus with nonbelievers by our many responsibilities, pressures, and interests.

It is crucial that Christians—both individually and collectively—refocus our priority to reach out in Christ's name.†

Be Looking for Opportunities

What, then, is your assignment? It is to discover every person for whom you are responsible and to share Jesus with that person at the point of his or her deepest need.

For whom are you responsible? Every person you meet! If you have the opportunity to choose the topic of conversation, you will want to direct it toward Jesus. You influence each one—by what you say or do not say, by what you do or fail to do. Ezekiel was designated by the Lord as a "watchman" to those about him. He was accountable to "speak to warn the wicked." If he did not and if they died in their sin, their blood would be on his hands (3:17–19). He was responsible for being faithful in sharing God's message with them—whether they listened or not!

We, too, are responsible for sharing the good news of salvation and for the spirit in which we deliver it. The response of the listener is not the deciding factor in whether or not we give them the message. It is the mandate of our Master to take the Gospel to every person.

The word *witness* in the New Testament is closely akin to the term *watchman* in the book of Ezekiel. Every Christian is a watchman and a witness. Our job is to share; God's job is to bring the results. Our job is sow the seed; God's job is to give the harvest. You can depend on God to do His job. He desires that none should perish, but that all should come to repentance. But He uses people to reach other people with the Gospel. He has called every Christian to share Jesus. And those whom the Lord calls, He equips and empowers. He has called us to be faithful, not necessarily to be successful in bringing others to Him.

Opportunities Are Everywhere

Who should be the focus for your witness? D. L. Moody, famed evangelist, said, "I see every person I meet as though he had a huge *L* in the middle of his forehead. I consider him lost until I know he is saved." With whom are you to share Jesus? Everyone you meet!

You cannot share with the wrong person. Every person you meet is either united with Christ or is without Christ. If you witness to a believer, you will have found a new brother or sister. You can rejoice together. You can encourage him or her in the Lord. If the believer is already a member of another church, you can urge him to be faithful and fruitful in that place of service. Some will accept Christ and go to a church other than your own. This, too, is positive. The Holy Spirit will guide the person into the church where he or she can grow.

In Seoul, Korea, I was going through customs. I could not speak Korean, but I had with me a witnessing booklet, "Steps to Peace with God," by Billy Graham, printed in English and Korean. I knew that many Koreans would recognize his name due to the crusades Mr. Graham has conducted there. So I asked the first Korean I met (a customs official), "May I share with you about Jesus Christ? This booklet written by Billy Graham tells how you can know Christ personally." A smile spread across his face. In broken English, he said, "I Christian too." He extended his hand and warmly welcomed me to Korea. What a joy that the first person I met on the other side of the earth was a brother. But I would have missed that joy if I had not shared Jesus with him.

If you discover that the person is an unbeliever, the message you share is even more necessary. It may be a harvest encounter in which the person accepts Christ or a seed-sowing encounter where the seed of the Gospel is received, only to take root and grow. Regardless of which type of encounter it is, you can depend on the Holy Spirit to use your witness. You may not lead that person to the Lord at the time, but you may be sure you are providing a road map to Him.

I was in an office building one day, bending over the lavatory in a rest room, washing my face after visiting with a friend who worked in the building. I was due to preach in a church nearby in a few minutes. Suddenly I realized that I was not alone. A man was standing at the other side of the room with a mop in his hand. The impression came, *Witness to him.* I put up an argument, *Oh, this isn't a good time. We're in the rest room.* Again I felt a nudge from the Holy Spirit. *Witness to him.* Again I argued mentally, *But I don't have time. I have to be at the church soon.* Then came the clincher: *You may be the last Christian he will meet before he stands in the presence of God.*

Realizing my responsibility before God for this man, I wiped the water from my face with a towel and turned to him. "Friend, may I ask you a question?" Now this is not my usual method of witnessing. But moved by the urgent leading of the Holy Spirit, I asked directly and almost abruptly, "Are you a saved man?" I didn't know if he even knew what I was talking about.

Just as directly as I had asked, he replied, "No, but I would like to be!" And within five minutes, he had prayed and received Christ as his Savior. Briefly I told him the next steps to take. He promised that the following Sunday he would tell the pastor of the church he sometimes attended that he had trusted Christ as Lord and Savior.

I left, shaking my head at the ways of God. In a rest room of all places! A cold-turkey direct witness by one who was resisting the Holy Spirit's prompting to share Jesus! In such a brief time! How could it be? All I can say is that the Holy Spirit had prepared the way and his heart was ready to receive the message.

As one man has said, "There is no bad way to lead people to Jesus!" God uses all kinds of methods to bring all kinds of people to Christ in all kinds of places.

Do you know why many do not receive the forgiveness and new life Christ offers them? Because nobody has asked them! Just ask and let the Holy Spirit lead.

Opportunities Are Divine Appointments

Our loving Father arranges divine appointments for us to share Jesus often and in all kinds of places. A divine appointment is when the path of an obedient witness crosses the path of a person seeking God. Obedient witnesses are available to the Holy Spirit and sensitive to the people they meet.

The question is, "How do you know if one is a seeker?" They do not wear a name tag saying, "Seeker, share with me!" You have to look for an open door to share Jesus. (In Chapter 4, we will show how to gently guide a conversation to Jesus and lead a person to faith in Christ.) When you start to share Jesus in a conversation, however, you may probe ask questions, and share, always as the Holy Spirit leads. If the door opens, share Jesus to the extent of that person's receptivity. If one door remains closed, do not attempt to force it open. Try another door! Use a different approach. (I'll show you how in Chapters 10 and 11.) If the person is seeking God, he or she will respond, and you can share Jesus. If not, commit the person to the Holy Spirit and *leave the results to God.*

A Divine Appointment

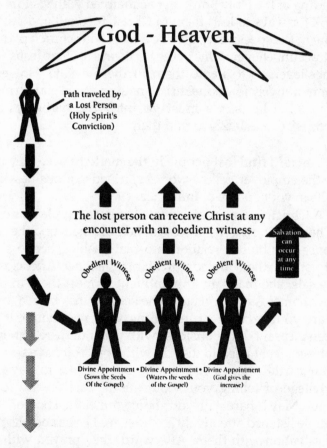

Remember, you have not successfully shared until you have shared Jesus with a person.

Be Alert for the Lost

Where are the lost? To reach people who need Christ, you must find them. Even Jesus had to find the lost before saving them. He came *to seek* and to save the lost (Luke 19:10)! He went to where they were and gave them the truth they needed.

You *will* find lost people at church. As you follow the leading of the Holy Spirit, get acquainted with visitors and look for ways to lead them to Christ. Step out and participate in the special evangelistic events your church plans to attract unbelievers. One of the best ways to share Jesus with unbelievers is to invite them to these events. However, comparatively few non-Christians ever attend church meetings. Like Jesus, we must go into "the highways and hedges" (Luke 14:23) to find them.

You *will* find lost people in the marketplace. They may be the employer, fellow workers, friends, or business contacts in your sphere of influence.

A Christian real estate agent showed a couple a number of houses. During the process of helping them find the right house, she built a relationship that enabled her to share Christ with them in a nonthreatening manner. After closing the sale, she made an appointment to meet them in their new home. As they visited, she said, "It has been a joy to share your excitement in finding your new home. It has been pleasant doing business with you. But there's another subject I feel I need to discuss with you. You have secured your earthly home. It's lovely. But I'd like to have the privilege of telling you about another and even greater home. May I share with you about your eternal home?" The couple listened attentively as she shared Jesus and His plan of salvation with them. Afterward, they prayed with her and received Christ, making Him Lord of their lives and their new home.

You *will* find lost people among your everyday contacts. It may be a student or teacher at the school, a doctor or nurse in the hospital, a clerk at the store, an executive in his place of business, the attendant at the service station, the waiter at the restaurant, etc. Or a lost person may come to your door. The mail carrier, the plumber, the electrician, the pest exterminator, a door-to-door sales representative, or any person at all may turn out to be a divine appointment.

You *will* find lost people behind labels. Many lost people wear such labels as Baptist, Methodist, Catholic, Assemblies of God, and Church of God in Christ, among others. But just because they wear a religious label does not mean they have a personal relationship with Christ. When they say, "I am Baptist," they may mean, "My grandfather was a Baptist deacon, so I'm a Baptist." Or, "The two times in my life that I went to church, it was a Baptist church."

My friend Jerry said he always told those who invited him to church that he was Catholic, and they never brought up the subject again. But the first time a Christian asked him if he had come to know Jesus Christ in a personal way and went ahead to share the Gospel with him, he immediately accepted Christ and joined a church. Jerry told me that he had never been interested in church. But when the Christian asked him if it would be all right to share about Jesus, he was interested in Jesus. Like many today, Jerry was hiding behind a religious label. I'll show you how to get beyond the labels to reach people with the Gospel of Christ.

You *will* find lost people behind doors. They are behind the doors of houses, apartments, businesses, and other places. Many are isolated and lonely. Some are discouraged and defeated. Some have all but cut themselves off from the rest of the world.

Through their church's organized outreach, two women found a lonely woman in her apartment. Overcome by fear, the woman had shut herself in and ventured out only occasionally to buy groceries. One of the Christian women led her to Christ and helped her get involved in Bible study. The lonely lady followed Jesus and found an enriching, uplifting fellowship with believers. Having found Christ as her indwelling Savior and constant companion, her personality and entire life were transformed. Some people, like that lady, will never be reached unless Christians care enough to knock on their doors to find them.

A group of thirty believers in a downtown church participated in another organized outreach. One member was so excited with the results—leading another person to Christ—that he was ready to do it again as soon as possible. The pastor said, "Through the organized outreach, I learned a great deal about our community. Not only did the people not know anything about our church, they didn't even know it was here!" Individual members began to share with family members and friends. They started reaching out to get acquainted and attempted to share Jesus with all the people in the neighborhood. Consequently, many accepted Christ, and found a home in that church's nurturing community.

You *will* find lost people behind masks. Some of the masks are success, self-satisfaction, indifference to the Gospel, and materialism. People behind masks may put up a front of success and self-satisfaction, while their hearts are empty and searching. They may not be aware of their own need, or they may not admit it until someone cares enough to intentionally share Jesus with them.

You *will* find lost people behind barriers. Social barriers—wealth and affluence, poverty, failure, ignorance, and cultural differences—prevent many from trusting Christ. Someone must care enough to bridge the gap. Others are blocked by racial and language barriers. Some are blocked by institutional barriers—prisons, jails, nursing homes, and hospitals. The caring, sharing church will organize people into creative ministries to help them share Jesus with unbelievers.

You will reach people for Christ as you realize that you are empowered to share Jesus with every person. You will begin to see every person as lost until you know that he or she has a relationship with Christ. Do everything you can to help your church develop ministries for reaching every person in the community with the Gospel, equipping every believer to share Jesus. As you and your friends are equipped and encouraged to share Him, you will be sensitive to the spiritual state of others and seek to share Jesus with them.

As you meet people who need Jesus, add their names to your prayer list. Contact each person periodically. Through prayer, time together, and the work of the Holy Spirit, some of them will become open to learning about Jesus. Contact them more frequently, always being sensitive to share Jesus as the opportunity occurs. Contact the rest less frequently, but do so consistently. The Holy Spirit will do His work of drawing the person to Christ. He will use your caring contact, the sharing of God's Word, and prayer.

What sort of contacts can you make with those on your prayer and share list? Ask the person to have coffee or go fishing with you, or to play tennis or golf. Invite the person to a party or to church. Make a telephone call or visit him or her at work or at home. Be sensitive to needs and find out how you can help. Bake a loaf of homemade bread or a cake and take it by. Write notes on special occasions such as birthdays, holidays, anniversaries, special achievements, etc. Remember the person's special interests and clip articles from newspapers and magazines to send. Or jot a handwritten note occasionally just to say, "I was thinking of you." Developing various approaches to cultivate and to reach all kinds of people for Christ is one of the most joyful challenges you will ever face.

One by one, the people on your prayer and share list will trust Christ. Does this mean that you will no longer have a list? No! As these people accept Christ, God will burden *their hearts* for the needs of *their* families, friends, and acquaintances, and you will have the opportunity of becoming their *partner*. You will know the incredible joy and satisfaction of joining your new brother or sister in Christ in seeking to reach his or her sphere of influence for the Lord! Your list and blessing will continue to grow!

†The Total Church Life evangelism strategy is a recommended study for this purpose. Based on Acts 1:8, the study teaches how churches can help their neighbors hear the good news of forgiveness and freedom through faith in Christ. To really reach a community, the whole church needs to get involved. Your church is a community of believers, and you *can* reach your neighborhoods as each of you consistently shares Jesus.

Chapter Two: Personal Review Questions

1. Evaluate the general attitude held toward the lost in your community by your church by using the scale below (1 = Somebody else should go out to reach them — 10 = We must do everything possible to reach them).

   1 2 3 4 5 6 7 8 9 10

2. Evaluate your personal concern for the lost by using the scale below (1 = very little concern — 10 = affects the way I live every day).

   1 2 3 4 5 6 7 8 9 10

3. How can a person increase their interest for the lost? Do you believe that it is the assignment of every Christian to share Jesus?

4. How would you define a divine appointment? Can you think of any other divine appointment in Scripture?

Spheres of Sharing Influence

We must share in our spheres of influence.

1. What are your spheres of influence?
2. Develop a plan to communicate with people you encounter in your normal day-to-day spheres of influence.

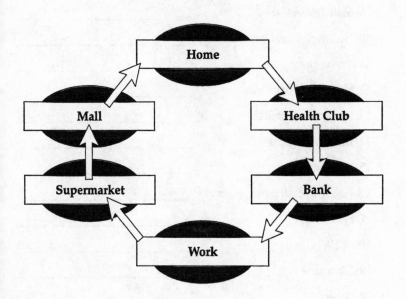

Casual Contacts

List as many for each category as you know. Identify them by placing a number by their names.

1. Bank Tellers _____

2. Service station attendants _____

3. Store clerks _____

4. Pharmacists _____

5. Doctors/Dentists _____

6. Waiters _____

7. Bus/taxi drivers _____

8. Delivery people _____

9. Mail deliverers _____

10. Health club professionals _____

11. Travel agent _____

12. Newspaper deliverers _____

13. Barbers/hair stylists _____

14. Insurance agents _____

15. Mechanics _____

16. Hobby or craft participants _____

17. Sports fans _____

18. Public officials _____

19. Librarians _____

20. Others _____

Family	Relatives
Friends	Work/School Associates
Neighbors	Other Contacts

Chapter 3

You *Can* Share Jesus with Confidence

You cannot reach *everyone* for Christ, but you can reach *someone*. You can share Jesus with those you meet. Some of them will trust Him as their Savior and Lord. Somebody reached you! Now you, with your unique personality and gifts, will be able to reach someone else. As you enter into partnership with Jesus and other Christians in naturally and consistently sharing the Gospel, every person can be reached with His message.

What could keep Christians from sharing Jesus? Motivated by love and the joy of being God's agent in reaching unbelievers and knowing the horrible consequence of unbelief, what could be so powerful as to keep us from witnessing at every possible opportunity? The primary reason for most of us is *fear*. The barrier of fear freezes us into silence. You can see it lurking in the following statements: "I'm afraid I may not know what to say." "I may fail." "What if I offend someone?"

The source of the problem with sharing Jesus is not somewhere out *there*! The problem is in *here*, in us. It is in our own attitudes and spirits. Still, it should not come as any surprise when the world and the devil attempt to intimidate us or shame us into silence in regard to witnessing.

37

That is exactly what happened among the early Christians. Through the fervent witness of Christians, thousands were being led to faith in Christ. Then Peter and John were arrested and forbidden to speak again in the name of Jesus. "Peter and John answered, 'Do you think God wants us to obey you or to obey him? We cannot keep quiet about what we have seen and heard'" (Acts 4:19–20).

When they were released, Peter and John met with the followers of the Lord and told them what had happened. Together they prayed, "Lord, listen to their threats! We are your servants. So make us brave enough to speak your message" (v. 29).

These early believers asked God for courage to share Christ no matter what happened or what they might suffer. "After they had prayed, the meeting place shook. They were all filled with the Holy Spirit and bravely spoke God's message" (v. 31).

The word translated "bravely" has been rendered "unhinderedly" in another translation. That which was within them was so great that they could not contain it. There was the free, unhindered flow of the Word of Christ to those who were lost. Their witnessing was not of the buttonholing, collar-grabbing, intimidating variety. They were simply being themselves, sharing what they had, the Lord Jesus, wherever they were with whomever they met.

Opposition can turn into *opportunity* to share Jesus as we pray, depend on Him, and continue to witness faithfully. Lost people need Christ. Many are open to the Gospel. Others will eventually become open. Fear can be overcome through an inner confidence given by our Lord. Every Christian can share with confidence. Confidence does not lie in our own ability, however, but in the Lord and in His principles.

God uses a mighty, threefold power team to open the hearts of unbelievers and bring them to Himself:

1. The Word of God
2. The Work of the Holy Spirit
3. The Witness of the Believer

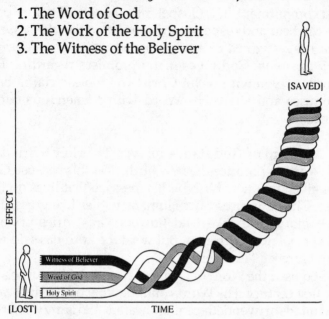

These three interact to bring lost people to a saving relationship with Christ

The principles are expressed in the account of the witness of the early church. "After they had prayed, the meeting place shook. They were all filled with the Holy Spirit and bravely spoke God's message" (Acts 4:31). The believers had been threatened and warned not to speak again in the name of Jesus. Instead of remaining silent, they came together in prayer, felt the shaking of the place where they were, and were filled with the Holy Spirit. That experience with God gave them confidence and they spoke up boldly, proclaiming God's Word. Many came to Christ.

The Word of God

The Word of God builds up our confidence to share. Be assured: God has never stopped powerfully using His Word to bring conviction, conversion, and commitment. The Gospel must be shared before people can hear and respond, and *inherent within the Gospel is power to rescue and redeem anyone, no matter how desperate their condition.* God gives many promises regarding His Word. As you witness for Christ you too can claim these promises and share His Word with tremendous confidence.

The Word of God stands forever. The Holy Spirit uses the Word to produce the new birth. "Do this because God has given you new birth by his message that lives on forever. The Scriptures say, 'Humans wither like grass, and their glory fades like wild flowers. Grass dries up, and flowers fall to the ground. But what the Lord has said will stand forever'" (1 Peter 1:23–25).

God used the Word of God to accomplish His purpose in the first century. His Word continues to work in the hearts and minds of twentieth-century hearers. "So is my word that goes out from my mouth: It will not return to me empty, / but will accomplish what I desire and achieve the purpose for which I sent it" (Isa. 55:11 NIV).

The Word of God burns out impurities. It melts the coldest heart and warms the soul of even the most resistant sinner. Like fire, it cleanses and purifies. And like a hammer that crushes rock, it smites the heart of the sinner with conviction and brings repentance. "'Is not my word like a fire,' declares the LORD, 'and like a hammer that breaks a rock in pieces?'" (Jer. 23:29 NIV).

The Word of God is the sword of the Spirit. "The sword of the Spirit, which is the word of God" (Eph. 6:17 NIV) pierces deep into the heart and mind of a person to bring conviction. Human counsel can give direction and guidance, but the Word of God penetrates to the spirit level of a life. It judges the thoughts and attitudes of the heart. It converts and regenerates. "What God has said is not only alive and active! It is sharper than any double-edged sword. His word can cut through our spirits and souls and through our joints and marrow, until it discovers the desires and thoughts of our hearts. Nothing is hidden from God! He sees through everything, and we will have to tell him the truth" (Heb. 4:12–13).

The Word of God builds faith. It reveals Christ and His salvation. The statement is sometimes made by well-meaning persons, "I intend to examine all the religions, then determine which religion is true and which I will accept." While Christianity stands up favorably in this kind of comparative investigation, faith in the living Christ grows in the human heart through hearing and receiving the truth of God's Word. So do whatever you can to expose people to the Word of God, for "faith comes from hearing the message, and the message is heard through the word of Christ" (Rom. 10:17 NIV).

The Word of God is His powerful way to save. The Gospel of Christ is inbreathed with the mighty, life-changing power of God. It is universal in its scope. Regardless of the people—group, race, nationality, or culture—the Gospel of Christ is God's relevant saving power to deliver from sin and change the life. "I am proud of the good news! It is God's powerful way of saving all people who have faith, whether they are Jews or Gentiles" (Rom. 1:16).

The Word of God produces commitment to Christ. The redeeming Gospel of Christ, when it is heard, generates faith-commitment in the heart. "But these are written so that you will put your faith in Jesus as the Messiah and the Son of God. If you have faith in him, you will have true life" (John 20:31).

41

The Word of God provides direction for living. Being born again is just the initial experience of salvation. It begins the process of the Christian life that ultimately climaxes when the believer is glorified in heaven. God's Word is adequate to direct your life in growth toward Christlikeness on this earth. "Everything in the Scriptures is God's Word. All of it is useful for teaching and helping people and for correcting them and showing them how to live" (2 Tim. 3:16–17).

The Word of God, shared from a heart of deep compassion, produces a harvest. By now the importance of planting the seed of God's Word in the minds and hearts of those about us should be clear. After all, within the seed of the Word is the germ of spiritual life with potential for harvest. But the germ must be watered with tears of compassion and concern by the sower. One Sunday morning, after a service marked by tears of concern and repentance, someone noted, "Pastor, you know, where there are no tears, there is no joy."

"Those who sow in tears will reap with songs of joy. / He who goes out weeping, carrying seed to sow, / will return with songs of joy, carrying sheaves with him" (Ps. 126:5–6 NIV).

You can share Jesus with confidence. The Word you share will be incredibly powerful in bringing others to Christ. The truth sets people free!

The Work of the Holy Spirit

As a witness for Christ, you are not alone in your desire and efforts to bring others to Him. God cares more about the person to whom you are witnessing than you do. "The Lord isn't slow about keeping his promises, as some people think he is. In fact, God is patient, because he wants everyone to turn from sin and no one to be lost" (2 Peter 3:9). Paul wrote to Timothy: "God wants everyone to be saved and to know the whole truth, which is, There is only one God, and Christ Jesus is the only person who can bring us humans to God. Jesus was truly human, and gave himself to rescue all of us humans. God showed us this at the right time" (1 Tim. 2:4–6).

The Holy Spirit both convicts the lost and inspires confidence for witness. Humanly speaking, this confidence is an impossibility! For a person to come to Christ, there must be the proper heart condition—repentance from sin and faith in the Lord Jesus Christ. No matter how adept one may be in witnessing, no human can give someone else the heart condition essential for salvation. It is the Holy Spirit who works to develop it through His convicting ministry.

God is *always* at work through His Spirit in the life of *every* person. Anytime you witness, you can be confident that the Holy Spirit was there beforehand and is now doing His work within the person's heart and mind. After you are through, the Holy Spirit will *still* be there, working to save that person.

The Holy Spirit works on two fronts at the same time. When a Christian shares Jesus, the Holy Spirit works to enable the believer to share the mighty Word of God. At the same time, He works in the life of the unbeliever, moving the person toward conversion.

Christians witnessed with confidence in Acts 4:31 when they prayed and were filled with the Holy Spirit. "After they had prayed, the meeting place shook. They were all filled with the Holy Spirit and bravely spoke God's message." Effective witnessing includes the Christian both *living* the life and *sharing* the Lord. Living under the control of the Holy Spirit is the key to both. The Holy Spirit enables the life of the believer to produce the fruit of the Spirit. Out of such a life flows a witness that the Holy Spirit can use in a maximum way. The following chapters will show how to use varied approaches in naturally guiding a conversation and sharing Jesus with others.

The Holy Spirit empowers the church. "The Holy Spirit will come upon you and give you power. Then you will tell everyone about me in Jerusalem, in all Judea, in Samaria, and everywhere in the world" (Acts 1:8). God's mission for His church is to witness to every person, beginning in the community and extending in an ever-enlarging circle to the ends of the earth.

Yet it is estimated that an average of no more than 3 to 5 percent of church members ever share Jesus with others. It is little wonder that churches lack spiritual vitality when they place low priority or no emphasis at all on reaching people for Christ. When 95 to 97 percent of the members of a church live in perpetual disobedience to the primary mission of Christ, how could there be a climate of spiritual awakening? Obedience to the commission of its Lord in Spirit-filled witness, along with prayer and unity, is essential to spiritual vitality in a church.

The Holy Spirit leads the believer to cross the paths of those who need Christ. He generates divine appointments for sharing Jesus. But sensitivity to witnessing opportunities and to people is of primary importance. The faithful Spirit-filled believer will be intentional in seeking opportunities to share Christ. Instead of passively waiting for an opening, the intentional witness will probe the possibilities, trusting the Holy Spirit to open the door at the appropriate time.

Philip's witness to the treasurer of the queen of Ethiopia is an excellent example: "Then Philip ran up close [to the chariot] and heard the man reading aloud from the book of Isaiah. Philip asked him, 'Do you understand what you are reading?'" (Acts 8:30). Philip approached the Ethiopian official with the intent of sharing Jesus with him. The Holy Spirit led Philip so that the timing was precisely right for him to cross the path of the Ethiopian caravan in an unpopulated desert. Coincidence? No! It was a God-directed incident—a divine appointment.

Philip could have let the caravan pass without making any effort to witness. He could have concluded that these people were strangers whom he would never meet again. He would certainly have no opportunity to follow up since they were traveling through the country. But Philip was committed to reaching every person with the Gospel. In fact, he was the first after Pentecost to take the Gospel to the Samaritans (Acts 8:4–8). God used him to expand the vision of the Jerusalem church to share the Gospel with every creature (vv. 14–25).

As we have seen, while the Holy Spirit empowers the Christian for witness, He also works in the lives of unbelievers to prepare them for the witness. In the case of the Ethiopian official, the Holy Spirit had cultivated his heart through contacts in Jerusalem. And when the official encountered Philip, he was already seeking the Lord, reading from a scroll written by the prophet Isaiah. Confidence for witness comes when you realize that you are working in partnership with the Holy Spirit and with other Christians who share Jesus.

The Holy Spirit guides us when we share Jesus. One of the barriers to witnessing is the fear of not knowing what to say. This is a legitimate concern. It is the reason for training, equipping, and preparation. It is important to study the Bible, to learn scriptural presentations of the Gospel, and to master the dynamics of sharing. Regardless of how much knowledge one has attained, however, it is impossible to anticipate the various situations and questions you will face in sharing Jesus. Witnessing is a dynamic and different encounter with each person. Trusting the Holy Spirit is imperative. Jesus promised, "Don't worry about . . . what you will say. At that time the Holy Spirit will tell you what to say" (Luke 12:11b–12). "Because of me, you will be dragged before rulers and kings to tell them and the Gentiles about your faith. But when someone arrests you, don't worry about what you will say or how you will say it. At that time you will be given the words to say. But you will not really be the one speaking. The Spirit from your Father will tell you what to say" (Matt. 10:18–20).

If you will step out and share Jesus in faith, the Holy Spirit will use you as His human instrument. "The fruit of the righteous is a tree of life, / and he who wins souls is wise" (Prov. 11:30 NIV). Through His Spirit, He will supernaturally compensate for your inadequacy. But bringing people to Christ is a Holy Spirit work. As a witness, you are the human instrument, but the Holy Spirit is the winner of souls. Jesus said, "No one can come to me unless the Father who sent me draws him" (John 6:44 NIV). You and I cannot bring anyone to faith in the Lord Jesus. The Father through the Holy Spirit must draw a nonbeliever to Christ.

For several weeks, Christian friends had patiently shared the Gospel with Kevin. His Sunday school teacher had also witnessed to him. Each time he was asked to consider making his decision for Christ, he courteously but firmly refused. Realizing that the Holy Spirit would continue to work in his life, one of his friends waited for three or four months before bringing up the subject again.

On Easter Sunday, Kevin came to church. One night during the next week, the Christian friend was impressed to drop by Kevin's home. Kevin began to talk about the Easter service and what Jesus did at the cross. It was obvious that the Holy Spirit was drawing him to Christ. That night he joyfully and simply repented of his sin and accepted Christ. He quickly led one of his closest friends to Christ. Humanly, it is impossible to win people to Christ, but cooperating with the Holy Spirit, we can guide them through the conversion experience.

The ministry of the Holy Spirit focuses on Jesus. The Spirit's purpose is to magnify and glorify Him. Jesus said that the Holy Spirit "will bring glory to me by taking my message and telling it to you" (John 16:14). The Holy Spirit revealed Jesus to Kevin. It was as if a light had been turned on in his heart and mind. God enlightened Kevin's mind and guided him into the truth that he had not realized before (v. 13).

Jesus promised that the Holy Spirit "will convict the world of guilt in regard to sin and righteousness and judgment: in regard to sin, because men do not believe in me; in regard to righteousness, because I am going to the Father, where you can see me no longer; and in regard to judgment, because the prince of this world now stands condemned" (vv. 8–11 NIV).

Ann, a brilliant young corporate executive assistant, was caught up in a hedonistic lifestyle. She became involved in an affair with her boss, a married man. One Sunday, while visiting a nearby church, she heard a sermon—"The Seventh Commandment: Adultery"—in a series of sermons on the book of Exodus. The Holy Spirit worked in such a way that she was present to hear just the right word directed to her need. She quietly slipped out after the service.

A few weeks later, at midnight, Ann's mother, who lived in another city, called Fred, a Christian acquaintance, and asked him to go to Ann's apartment immediately and try to help her. She said that Ann was ill and very disturbed and had no one to whom she could turn.

The situation appeared so urgent that Fred agreed but called two other Christians to go with him to Ann's apartment. When they arrived, they found that Ann had come under such heavy conviction by the Holy Spirit that guilt and fear of judgment had almost paralyzed her. She was afraid to drive to work. She was physically sick and mentally and emotionally almost at the breaking point.

Fred shared the Word of God about repentance, confession of sin, commitment to Christ, God's forgiveness, and delivering power with her. Ann confessed her sin and committed her life to Christ. She immediately experienced a glorious release and transformation. The three Christian friends then took her to the hospital for emergency medical care. She recovered quickly and was released. She continued to grow spiritually.

After some time, Ann met and married a committed Christian man. God used their lives to reach and disciple many for Christ. Their home became a center of redemptive love and witness for Christ.

Ann's experience is a living testimony to the reality of the Holy Spirit's conviction of sin, of the need for Christ, and of the certainty of judgment. She came to know Christ through the ministry of the Word of God, the work of the Holy Spirit, and the witness of believers.

The Holy Spirit enables believers to live victoriously.
During their lunch break at work, Ron shared Christ with his friend Jim. Jim was hesitant. "I can't accept Christ. I'm afraid I could never change and live the Christian life."

"You're right," his friend agreed. "You can't live it. I can't live it, either. This is a Holy Spirit work. If you could live it, you wouldn't need Jesus. When you receive Christ, two things happen. One, He forgives all your sin. Now, if He forgave your sin and left you like you are, you would, more than likely, go on in the same old way. But He doesn't leave you like you are. The second thing He does is give you the Holy Spirit, who changes you within. He gives you a new life, a new direction, a new desire, and strength you never had before. The question is 'Are you trusting Jim or Jesus?'"

The light broke through. Jim yielded his life to Christ, was born again, and was later baptized. He began to live a quality of life for Christ that he was never able to live before. Depending on the Holy Spirit and obeying His leadership gives the confidence needed, both for effective witnessing and for living the Christian life.

It is the Holy Spirit who transacts the new-birth experience and gives spiritual life. All of the facets of His work are stated by Jesus in His word to Nicodemus: "I tell you the truth, unless a man is born again, he cannot see the kingdom of God. . . . I tell you the truth, unless a man is born of water and the Spirit, he cannot enter the kingdom of God. Flesh gives birth to flesh, but the Spirit gives birth to spirit" (John 3:3, 5–6 NIV).

The Witness of the Believer

Realizing that God uses the witness of the believer to reach people for Christ gives confidence for sharing Jesus. People reach people. Apart from believers sharing the Word of God in the power of the Holy Spirit, people do not usually come to Christ.

Believers sharing their faith is an integral part of God's plan for reaching the lost for Christ. When Jesus revealed the coming of the Holy Spirit and His ministry to His disciples, He indicated that both the *witness* of the Holy Spirit and the *witness* of His disciples are essential to His plan: "I will send you the Spirit who comes from the Father and shows what is true. The Spirit will help you and will tell you about me. Then you will also tell others about me, because you have been with me from the beginning" (John 15:26–27).

Jesus is calling for laborers to enter the harvest field to reap what His Spirit has sown. "'My food,' said Jesus, 'is to do the will of him who sent me and to finish his work. Do you not say, "Four months more and then the harvest"? I tell you, open your eyes and look at the fields!

They are ripe for harvest. Even now the reaper draws his wages, even now he harvests the crop for eternal life, so that the sower and the reaper may be glad together. Thus the saying "One sows and another reaps" is true. I sent you to reap what you have not worked for. Others have done the hard work, and you have reaped the benefits of their labor'" (John 4:34–38 NIV).

Jesus set forth the principle of partnership in sharing the Gospel for His followers. The Holy Spirit may use a number of people to share Jesus with an unbeliever before someone finally leads that unbeliever to saving faith. God uses everyone who shares Jesus. The believer witnesses. God gives the harvest. Paul said, "I planted the seed, Apollos watered it, but God made it grow" (1 Cor. 3:6 NIV).

God could have chosen any means He desired to reach people with the Gospel. He chose to use those who have experienced what they share. In Acts 10 the Roman centurion, Cornelius, is described as a devout man who prayed and sought God. Since God always responds to a seeking heart, He sent an angel to Cornelius. The angel did not tell him how to trust Christ, but directed him to seek out Simon Peter who would tell him what to do to receive Him.

At that time, the church in Jerusalem, including Peter, did not fully understand the extent of Christ's commission. They could not visualize Gentiles being included in the redemptive work of Christ. Remember, however, what you have learned about how God works. He not only works to draw the person to Christ, but He also prepares the witness. He began to prepare Peter to bear witness to Cornelius while He was responding to Cornelius's seeking heart. You can be confident that God will do the same for you as you seek to share Jesus with others.

God gave Peter a vision while he slept. In this vision, He let down a sheet from heaven filled with all kinds of animals. A voice spoke and said, "Get up, Peter. Kill and eat" (Acts 10:13 NIV). Though Peter was hungry, he would not, considering the animals unclean. The voice spoke again, "Do not call anything impure that God has made clean" (v. 15). While Peter meditated on the meaning of the vision, messengers from Cornelius arrived, asking for Peter. Peter interpreted the vision to be God's instruction for him to take the Gospel to Cornelius. The Gentile, Cornelius, and his household responded to the Gospel.

The angel could have shared the plan of salvation with Cornelius, but sharing the Gospel is not the ministry of angels. The assignment to share Jesus with the lost was given by our Lord to every believer. Sharing Jesus naturally grows out of the personal experience of the individual believer with Christ Himself.

Non-Christians need people who have experienced new life to guide them through conversion. When Philip encountered the Ethiopian official who was reading from Isaiah 53, he asked, "'Do you understand what you are reading?' The official answered, 'How can I understand unless someone helps me?'" (Acts 8:30–31). That was Philip's cue to explain the Gospel to this seeker.

Those without Christ are spiritually blind. They need someone to show them the way to Christ. Saul of Tarsus is a classic example. Those who stoned Stephen laid their clothes at Saul's feet (Acts 7:58). A great persecution against the church broke out that day. No doubt Stephen's testimony made a great impression on Saul, however, for on his way to arrest and imprison believers in Damascus, he was blinded by a light from heaven. There on the road, he experienced the risen Lord. Jesus told Saul to go into Damascus and he would be told what to do. Then Jesus appeared to Ananias and told him to look for Saul and give him instruction. Although he was evidently not prominent among the disciples, Ananias was used by God to baptize and give guidance to the one chosen to be the great apostle to the Gentiles. Ananias was an available witness. God can use any believer who makes himself available.

God uses a team of three to reach people for Christ. Without the Word of God and the Work of the Holy Spirit, the spiritually dead cannot find life in Christ. But it also takes the faithfulness of believers who desire to reach the lost. When few believers in the church are obediently sharing Jesus, the Holy Spirit's power is quenched and few people come to Christ. But in any assembly where the members are obedient to the Holy Spirit and are equipped to share Jesus and participate in the organized outreach, many will come to Christ. A spirit of revival will continuously permeate that body.

You, as a believer, are a vital part of God's team to lead others to Christ. You can share with confidence. It is your assignment as a Christian. He has given you spiritual gifts to use for witness and ministry. God would *never* require a thing of you and not equip and enable you to do it. You are different from every other person. Your unique personality and gifts can be used by God to reach those around you for Christ. You can develop the individual style of sharing Jesus that fits many an unsaved person and situation, since unbelievers, too, are all different. For each of them there is a Christian who can be used by God to share Jesus with each one. As we faithfully witness to lost people, many will dedicate their lives to following Christ.

Chapter Three: Personal Review Questions

1. In Acts 4:29 why do you think that Peter and John prayed for more confidence for their witness of Jesus?

2. The team of three God uses in the mission of sharing Jesus are the Word of God, the work of the Holy Spirit,

and the witness of the believer. What part does each play in the work of evangelism?

3. Think of one way a believer can find confidence in the team connection with the Word of God? With the Holy Spirit?

4. What are some of the everyday questions of life which make natural opportunities for sharing the truth of the Word of God?

5. Acts 1:8 promises that all Christians will receive power from the Holy Spirit to be the witness of Jesus. What kind of power have we received?

Chapter 4

You *Can* Share Jesus in a Nonthreatening Way

People Sharing Jesus is a Christ-centered, other-centered approach to witnessing. Focusing on the individual and his or her situation, needs, and interests is key. To share Jesus relationally and conversationally breaks down barriers and builds up rapport. Further, sharing Jesus in this way is nonthreatening, both to the Christian who is sharing and to the person with whom Jesus is being shared.

Trying to force a Gospel presentation only results in tension for everyone involved. Using pressure often results in defensiveness in the non-Christian. Many have been able to overcome this tension to become effective. But for others, *People Sharing Jesus* is an alternative approach.

The purpose of this chapter is to help you learn how to use a conversation guide in sharing Christ with any person you meet at the point of that person's unique need. This guide will help you share Jesus in the least threatening way possible. You can use this guide spontaneously in a sharing conversation in the marketplace or in a more formal encounter in a person's home or office. What I'm about to share is not a theory. Conversational witnessing has been used by people in all walks of life to share Jesus in schools, airplanes, health clubs, restaurants, hospitals, and many other places.

Since God's assignment to you is to share Jesus with every possible person, you can be sure of two things. *First,* you will *never* meet a person God does not love (John 3:16). *Second,* you will *never* meet a person God does not want to bring to Himself. "The Lord isn't slow about keeping his promises, as some people think he is. In fact, God is patient, because *he wants everyone to turn from sin and no one to be lost*" (2 Peter 3:9).

The message of the Gospel is the same for all people. When you share the Good News about Jesus, however, you need to avoid a rigid, cookie-cutter approach to everyone. Each person is unique, with a different background and distinct needs. Be tactful and considerate in sharing Jesus with others. The key is simple: *approach each person with respect and love.*

You can learn much about sharing Jesus through your local church. But God can use you to share Jesus even if you lack formal training in techniques. As you share from a sincere and caring heart what Christ has done for you, the Holy Spirit will bless your witness.

Every unbeliever desperately needs someone to share Jesus with tact, love, and courtesy at the point of his or her deepest need. Never forget that! They need you—or more to the point, they need to hear the message you have. Surface needs of individuals—social, relational, physical, financial, mental, and emotional—will vary. The caring Christian will certainly want to minister to these surface needs. But the deepest need, a relationship with Jesus Christ, is the same for every person. An intimate and growing relationship with Him is the *foundation* for resolving life's other problems and needs.

It is often wise to begin by meeting a surface need and then go on to share Christ at the point of the deepest need. Unbelievers may be affluent or living in poverty, educated or uneducated, religious or nonreligious, moral or immoral—as different as people can be. Simply and naturally guiding a conversation with an unbeliever helps get beyond these surface issues to the real spiritual need.

Using a conversation guide will allow the Holy Spirit to help you create an openness to the message of Christ on the part of the person you are trying to reach. On the other hand, a pressure approach may result in that person making a premature decision to trust Christ without experiencing genuine repentance and conversion. It may also elicit barriers of defensiveness and resistance to the witness.

Late one afternoon I found myself reacting defensively to a salesperson who came to my home at a very inconvenient time. The man insisted on coming in to present his product. I wanted to be courteous, but I had only thirty minutes before having to leave for an appointment. I invited him in after telling him that I could give him twenty-five minutes. But he insisted on making his entire presentation. He talked continuously, though I never heard a word. I was thinking how to say no when he was finished! You may experience the same kind of result if you do all the talking rather than listening and sharing Jesus in two-way communication. Remember: you don't have a product to sell—you have a person to share.

The nonthreatening conversational approach to sharing Christ involves listening as much or more than speaking. The believer guides the conversation so that a discussion of spiritual things is introduced quite naturally. It should be noted, however, that there is no single best approach in personally sharing the Gospel. When the Holy Spirit is leading, you may sometimes find yourself sharing very directly, even abruptly.

An outstanding Christian friend of mine gave his testimony of coming to Christ through the brief, direct, and abrupt sharing of a nervous young believer. He was even offended by the witness, but the Holy Spirit used it anyway. It happened when he was a soldier on leave. He was sitting at a drugstore counter ordering a Coke when the soda fountain attendant blurted out, "Are you a Christian?"

Infuriated, the soldier left his Coke on the counter and

stormed out of the store. But the question "Are you a Christian?" continued to haunt him. And two weeks later he went to church and received Christ. The converted soldier never saw the enthusiastic young believer again. And this side of heaven, that attendant may never know the effect of his witness. But God does use the Spirit-led witness of His people, regardless of how inadequate it may seem.

The guide for drawing out a person in conversation, removing barriers, and creating an openness to consider the Gospel may be remembered by using an acronym:

F — Family
I — Interests
R — Religion
M— Message

Use the **F** for family as a reminder to discuss the person's family and background. The **I** is a reminder to converse about the person's interests. **R** for religion reminds you to dialogue about the person's religious background and interests. You may share briefly something of your own background and experience with Jesus. The **M** is for Message. You will continue the conversation and share the Gospel with the person.

The Conversation Guide

As you become comfortable with the conversation guide, you may vary its order to help the flow of the conversation. Whatever you do, don't be a slave to a rigid approach. Ask the Holy Spirit to lead.

Remember, your *motive* is important as well as your message, so use the conversation guide because you genuinely care about people. Be willing to listen more than you speak. And as you listen, you will begin to establish a relationship and better understand how to share the Gospel. The following are suggestions as to how you can utilize the conversation guide to engage in natural and friendly dialogue. As you share in conversation, ask questions to allow the person to tell his or her own story. Gently guide the conversation through the acronym **FIRM**.

F—Family

Most people enjoy talking about their family or background. Ask questions such as:

- Where did you grow up?

- Where are you from?

- Tell me about your family.

- How many children do you have?

- Where do you live?

Be a listener. Share naturally and with interest as the person talks about himself or herself. Then, gently move the conversation onto **Interests** by asking a leading question.

I—Interests

People also like to talk about what they do. Ask a young person about sports, school, and hobbies. Allow the person to share about his or her job, leisure-time activities, and long-term goals. Notice the books, magazines, pictures, or trophies in the home or office. Ask questions that will provide clues to the person's real purpose in life. If you know nothing about the particular interest expressed, do some research so you will be able to enter into a meaningful discussion next time you meet. And don't just ask questions. Respond to their responses. Be vulnerable if they are. This creates rapport. They begin to know you as you get to know them.

In a taxi in New York City, I got acquainted with the driver and learned that he lived on Staten Island. After we talked about his home and family, I asked him how long he had been driving taxis. He told me he had been driving for about ten years. Since he was already a middle-aged man, I asked, "Do you intend to drive a cab for the rest of your life?"

He was thoughtful for a moment before he replied, "I never thought about that."

"Did you know that God has a wonderful plan for every life?" I went on. Then, briefly, I shared Jesus with him. I told him that he might be a cab driver for the rest of his life, but that God could use him as a missionary right in his cab as he met people from all over the world. He told me what he understood about what a missionary is and does. We discussed how he could share Jesus as he drove people to and from the airport.

At the back of the cab, as we unloaded luggage on a busy street in Manhattan, the cab driver bowed his head and prayed, expressing repentance and receiving Christ. As I walked away, he shouted, "Hey! Mister!" I turned and he smilingly said, "You know that missionary you talked about? I'm going to be that missionary!"

Talking with a man about his job opened the door for me to share Christ with him.

R—Religion

After you know a little about the person's family, job, or interests, introduce the topic of religion; move the subject of the conversation to church. This will guide the conversation toward the point where you can share the message of the Gospel naturally. If there is too abrupt a transition in the conversation, you may alarm the person and they'll erect defenses.

Approach what you want to talk about gently, cautiously. You don't want to spook the person.

Try asking: "What's your religious background? What church do you attend? Is there a church in your neighborhood? Do you often think about spiritual things?"

Use the creativity the Holy Spirit gives you to introduce the subject of **Religion**. In conversation with an engineer from Arkansas, Scott said, "Being from President Clinton's state, you're probably a Baptist. Most of the people I've met from Arkansas have been Baptists."

He laughed, "You're almost right. There are a lot of Baptists in Arkansas, but not me. I'm a _____" (indicating his background).

Once he had identified his church relationship, the conversation moved beyond that and Scott discussed his spiritual background and his hunger for meaning in life with him. From that point, the message of the Cross flowed naturally as Scott enjoyed the privilege of sharing Jesus with him.

So, why talk about religion in this conversation? For two reasons:

One, it identifies where the person is spiritually.

Two, it bridges the gap between where the person is in his everyday thinking over to where he considers his spiritual life to be. Most people when you meet them will not be thinking consciously in spiritual terms. They will be thinking in terms of the secular. The secular is not necessarily evil but simply nonspiritual. Most of us, most of the time, walk around thinking about business or jobs or finances or family or sports or problems—whatever, you name it. As one who cares and shares about Jesus, your goal is to lead them to consider the message of Jesus in the least threatening way possible. Church is a neutral subject that almost any person can comfortably talk about. They may talk positively about the church, or they may talk negatively. It doesn't matter. What does matter is that the subject of church in general can bridge the gap between the secular and the spiritual in your conversation.

The Following Diagram Illustrates:

**The Gap that must be bridged.
Church most neutral, least
threatening topic.**

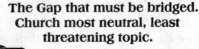

Secular

Realm where most people
are thinking, talking, acting,
living. Not necessarily evil,
merely non-spiritual
(Job, Ballgame, Etc...)

Spiritual

Realm into which you
guide their thoughts
of Christ.

M—Message

Move from a discussion of religion or church to sharing the Gospel using a transitional statement.

Transitional Statement: "We've been talking about church. But it's possible for a person to join every church ir town and still not know Jesus Christ. Knowing Jesus personally is what makes the difference"

Be sure not to be negative about a church or denomination, however. You may say, "When you have received Christ personally, you will want to be a part of His church. He commanded His people to be in fellowship with His

62

body, the church. But the most important thing is accepting Christ and committing your life to Him."

Most people will agree that the church cannot provide eternal life. And they will be happy to hear you confirm their opinion, whether they are religious or not.

Next, ask a key question. But get the person's permission before you do so they will not be offended. You may say, "May I ask you a personal question about this?" Very seldom, if ever, will you not be permitted to ask the question.

Key Question: "Have you come to know Jesus Christ in a personal way or would you say you are still in the process?"

The value of the question is apparent. It is nonthreatening both to the person asking the question and to the one being asked. It allows the person to whom you are witnessing to identify his or her position in a positive way. The person can say, "I'm in the process" without feeling trapped. It gives an opening for you to say, "Then you have been giving some thought to it?"

There are three possible answers to the question. Regardless of the answer, you can easily move on to present the message of Christ.

Three possible answers:

- "Yes."

Ask: "When and how did you come to know Him?"

Allow the person to share his or her conversion experience. If you doubt the experience or if it is unclear, you may ask, "May I share with you how I came to Christ?" Then present the plan of salvation. If the person's testimony is clear and certain, rejoice with him or her.

- "No."

Ask: "May I share with you how you can come to know Him?"

If the person refuses, discuss the cause of the reluctance. You may ask, "Do you mind sharing with me about your reluctance to discuss how to know Christ?"

If there is an openness, go on to share the message. Prayer at this point may open the way. If there is not time or for some reason you cannot go on with the witness, give the person a booklet or tract that explains how to receive Christ. Ask the person to read the booklet as soon as possible. Briefly explain the booklet and how to pray and receive Christ as time permits. Get the person's name, address, and phone number for follow-up. Leave your name and phone number for contact as interest develops.

- "Still in the process."

Ask: "Then you have given some thought to it. May I share with you how you can come to know Him personally?"

At this point, present the plan of salvation. Ask the Holy Spirit to guide. You may share your testimony, use *People Sharing Jesus* New Testament, John 3, the Roman Road, the Lifeline Illustration, a witnessing booklet, or whatever Scriptures God leads you to use.

How to Share with a Stranger

When Cliff flew into Las Vegas one night, he had a divine appointment with Eduardo at the airport. When the late evening flight arrived, not many people were left in the terminal. Cliff hurried to the auto rental counter. As Eduardo prepared the rental papers, Cliff guided the conversation to the subject of his relationship with Christ. It began as Cliff approached the counter.

Ed: "Hello, may I help you, sir?"

Cliff: "Sure. I need a car for the next four days while I am here for a meeting. Here is my reservation number. My name is Cliff. I notice by your name tag that yours is Ed."

Ed: "My name is Eduardo, but I go by Ed."

Cliff: "Ed, have you lived in Las Vegas long or have you come from somewhere else?" (Cliff is beginning the conversation by injecting a question about "F" for Family.)

Ed: "Oh, I have just been here for about two years. I am from the Philippines. I really miss home. All of my family is there, except my wife. She is here. My family is very close. We always get together for meals and to visit."

Cliff: "I know you miss your family a lot. What caused you to come to Las Vegas? Was it your job?" (Cliff is moving the conversation to a discussion of "I" for Ed's Interests.)

Ed: "I came for a job. Actually, I am trying to get a new start. In the Philippines I had a million dollars, but I lost it! Then all my friends turned away from me. I am working here to make a living and to try to start over, but it is tough. You see, now my wife has even left me. She is having an affair with another man. They have been living together, but I have persuaded her to come back and try again. So I am really at the bottom."

Cliff: "Man, I am terribly sorry. You really are having a tough time. In all of this have you felt the need of a strength greater than your own?" (Cliff is introducing the "R" for Religion.)

Ed: "I surely have. I need help!"

Cliff: "Then, may I ask you a personal question about this?" (Remember, if you get permission to ask the question, the person will not be threatened when you do.)

Ed: "Yes, you may."

Cliff: "Ed, have you come to know Jesus Christ in a personal way or would you say you are still in the process?"

Ed: "Cliff, I guess I am still in the process."

Cliff: "Then you have been giving some thought to it already. Is that true?"

Ed: "Yes, I have. In fact, it is interesting you brought this up. Just a few nights ago I was driving behind a car with the bumper sticker that said, 'SMILE, GOD LOVES YOU!' I said, 'Yes, God, I needed that!'"

Cliff: "Ed, I am about to ask you for a map to help me know how to get to where I want to go. But first, may I give you a map? It is entitled *Here's Hope.* It is about Jesus. It is laid out like a road map. It shows the road to come to know Christ, to live an abundant life here and to live with Christ in eternity. May I share it with you?" (Now Cliff is introducing the "M" for Message.)

Ed: "Yes, I need help! I am nothing but an alien here!"

Cliff held one side of the *Here's Hope* booklet and Ed held the other as they discussed what it said. Then, standing behind the counter, Ed trusted Christ. He bowed his head and prayed, asking God to forgive his sins and for Christ to come in and direct his life.

Cliff pointed out in the booklet the things Ed could do to grow in Christ and follow Him. Then Cliff said, "Ed, you said you are nothing but an alien here. I want to give you the name of a church where you can go and you will not be an alien there. You will be part of the family. You are now part of the family of God. They will love you there. If it is okay, I will give them your name and phone number to call."

Ed gave Cliff his phone number and said, "I really believe God sent you to me tonight."

How to Share with Someone You Know

The illustration cited above portrays a first-time witness encounter with a stranger. But the question may arise: "How can I approach someone I know very well, such as a friend, family member, a fellow worker in the marketplace, or someone with whom I have previously shared?"

Some general relational principles need to be regarded:

1. Be genuine in your communication.

2. Pray for the guidance of the Holy Spirit.

3. Convey a spirit of love, humility, and courtesy.

4. Avoid an attitude of condescension, judgment, and condemnation.

5. Ask for the person's permission.

Some possible approaches that may be used:

1. Use the conversation guide **FIRM**. Although you know the person well, you can still talk about family, interests, religion, and message. The conversation can be even more meaningful since you do already know one another. You may ask such questions as: "How are the children? Where do you plan to go on your vacation? How was your golf game Saturday?"

2. Use bridging statements and secure permission to discuss the person's religious life and to share about Jesus. Some possibilities I have used are as follows:

- "You and I have talked about our relationship with Christ at other times. Have you thought much about it lately? May we talk about it again?"

- "We know one another very well, but we've never discussed our relationship with God. May I ask you a question about that?" (Wait for a response.) "Have you come to know Jesus Christ in a personal way, or would you say that you are still in the process?"

- "I feel that I need to apologize to you. We're friends (or family), but I've never shared with you something very important to me—my Savior, Jesus. May I tell what He has done in my life?" (Wait for permission, then share your personal salvation testimony.) Then ask, "Have you come to know Jesus Christ in a personal way, or would you say you are still in the process?"

- "I've been thinking and praying lately about something very important to me—your relationship with Jesus. May I ask you a question about that?"

Person-centered witnessing is a two-way communication. It involves dialogue rather than monologue. The conversation guide will help in assessing the person's receptivity and can lead to a nonthreatening presentation of the Gospel.

Chapter Four: Personal Review Questions

Think through some questions you could use while following the **FIRM** conversation-guide approach in building rapport.

Family
1.
2.
3.
4.

Interests
1.
2.
3.
4.

Religion
1.
2.
3.
4.

Message (Take a preview look at Chapter 11 to stimulate your thinking on the transition question to the message of the Gospel.)

Section Two

You Have Been Entrusted to Share Jesus—With People

You will be more effective when you share Jesus if you are centered on the person you're sharing with. It involves two-way communication between the Christian and the non-Christian. It focuses on sharing Christ at the point of a person's particular need.

Message-centered sharing is the method of telling the plan of salvation in the same way each time. Some, whose hearts have already been prepared by the Holy Spirit, will be led to Christ using this approach. Others, however, will be turned off, or may not understand the message-centered witness. Perhaps you've seen this before and you've said, "Not me—if that's evangelism, forget it." Believe me, I know that feeling. The person-centered method I'm about to show you is *completely* different.

The person-centered witness is no less faithful to present the Gospel and the plan of salvation than is the message-centered witness. The difference is that the person-centered witness is careful to understand and start where the unbeliever is. Person-centered evangelism is so important because the very heart of the Good News of forgiveness and freedom through faith in Jesus is intensely personal.

Person-centered sharing sensitively enters into conversation with a person with the intention of sharing Jesus as the Holy Spirit directs. At some point the unbeliever must be confronted with the Gospel. No one drifts into salvation. People are converted to Christ by the power of the Gospel.

Sharing the Gospel should not be negative nor condemning. It is most effective when done relationally. The person-centered witness never shares from a position of self-righteousness, speaking down to the unbeliever. When you share Jesus in a person-centered way, you will experience the wonderful dynamic of a forgiven sinner sharing with an unforgiven sinner the love of Jesus Christ.

Sharing is both relational and intentional. It is not either/or; it is both/and. Your spirit and attitude is paramount and should be characterized by love for Jesus and love for the person with whom you are sharing. When you love Jesus and you love the person, you will do your best to bring the two together.

It should be your intent, as someone who shares Jesus in a person-centered way, to lead the unbeliever to Him as quickly as the Holy Spirit prepares the way. Meaningful relationships are essential to effective sharing. Developing a relationship to the point where you can lead someone to Jesus may require an extended time or a brief time. It may take as long as three months or three years, or as few as three minutes, depending on the receptivity of the individual and the work of the Holy Spirit.

Unfortunately, relationship building rather than intentionally sharing Jesus has become the focus of many Christians. Focusing on building a relationship rather than leading the lost to Christ presents two dangers. First, the longer one focuses on the relationship, the more difficult it is to present the Gospel message. As intimacy is developed, we often find it emotionally more difficult to risk disrupting the relationship by sharing the Gospel. The possibility is that the friend may become offended by the Gospel and the convicting work of the Holy Spirit. The longer the relationship continues and the more familiar we are with the person the less urgency we tend to have to share Jesus. People are not won to Christ by relationships with Christians. It is the Gospel of Christ that is the power of God for salvation (Rom. 1:16). Second, during the process of finding ways to build the relationship, time may run out. The non-Christian may die and go to hell, not knowing Christ. Sharing Jesus in a person-centered way means building the relationship while seeking to share Jesus as soon as possible.

Through giving attention to understanding the person with whom you are sharing, you will develop a relationship that will make your witness more effective. You will better understand how to approach him or her as you begin to share Jesus.

The chapters in Section 2 are a practical guide for understanding unbelievers and learning how to establish and build a relationship with them. In these chapters you will discover how to understand people, listen to them, and love them as God loves them. We'll focus on the condition of the lost as the Bible portrays it and they experience it. You will begin to recognize that those who don't know Christ are at different levels of spiritual understanding and development. Your confidence to share Jesus will be enhanced as you realize that every encounter with a person helps them more fully understand the Gospel and more deeply realize their need for Jesus.

Chapter 5

You Share Jesus with People Who Matter to God

People are primary! Jesus came for people. "God loved the people of this world so much that he gave his only Son, so that everyone who has faith in him will have eternal life and never die" (John 3:16).

It is marvelous that while our wonderful salvation is by divine initiative, it is intensely personal.

Salvation is personal. God transforms people one by one. Even in mass evangelism meetings, when many respond to the invitation to trust Christ, God deals with each one individually. The majority of people who come to Christ in crusades and evangelistic meetings have already had someone share with them personally about Jesus.

Sin is personal. To be rescued from sin, a person must become conscious of their own sins and how sin has separated them from God. The Holy Spirit convicts of sin as the Gospel of Christ is shared.

Repentance is personal. Godly sorrow for our sin leads us to repentance. Before we trusted Christ, it was the realization of how much God loves us in spite of our sinfulness that caused sorrow to well up in our hearts. (Rom. 4:4).

Repentance is the change of mind by which we make a U-turn from sin to God.

Faith is personal. Each of us, when we are brought to that place of repentance, must personally believe in Jesus Christ and receive Him as Savior and Lord. Person-centered witnessing takes into account the intensely personal experience of conviction of sin, repentance, and faith.

People Are Central to the Purpose of God

Intentional witnessing is most effective when it is person-centered. The purpose of *People Sharing Jesus* is to equip Christians to share the Lord Jesus with any person in any situation in a nonthreatening way at the point of their particular need. Understanding the heart, mind, and background of the one with whom you are sharing is an important facet of meaningfully sharing Jesus. Taking the initiative to *see people, hear people,* and *love people* will help you build a bridge of understanding to reach them for Christ.

So See People . . .

In this impersonal world with its explosive increase in population, we need to take the time to see people as God sees them. With our busy schedules, it is easy to pass people, speak to them, sit by them, or do business with them without ever seeing them.

Sharing Jesus is personal. It is realizing that everyone with whom we have contact is special. We see them as truly precious people who have significant lives, backgrounds, families, achievements, real problems, needs, joys, and sorrows. We see them through the eyes of God as persons for whom Christ died. We see them as people with tremendous potential for the kingdom of God.

In our concern with *how* to see people, it is important for us to consider how *not* to see them. The trend of a materialistic, self-centered society is to view them as objects to be exploited for selfish purposes.

. . . Not As a Means to an End

Some see people as things to be used. The self-centered, success-driven person often loves things and uses people. Interaction with people then becomes an effort to use them to get things or achieve goals. People become a means to an end. The people of God must care about the person. We must love people and use things for the benefit of people.

When we want to witness for Christ, we may be tempted to view the people on the receiving end of our witness as, well, almost as targets, as objects to be manipulated. We can be tempted into thinking of the people we meet in terms of our getting another notch on our "Gospel six-shooter." Does the person you witness to feel as though he is a victim of your attention rather than an object of Christ's love?

People, even lost people, are not stupid; they can spot a phony. When they sense the wrong motivation in us, they may refuse to open up to the Gospel of Christ. We must live so that unbelievers will believe that we really care about them before they are likely to believe anything else we have to offer.

. . . Not As Objects

Some see people as objects to be manipulated. Manipulative attitudes in Christians erect barriers rather than build bridges for the sharing of the Gospel. Some can even be manipulated into making a premature statement of faith in Christ. If this is done, it can become a barrier to the person's coming to a genuine experience of Christ as Savior and

Lord. Others will sense the wrong motivation of the person who has shared and refuse to be open to the glorious Gospel of Christ. Unbelievers need to realize that we really care about them.

One caring Christian at a social event questioned a lovely woman about her salvation. As they shared, she was deeply moved. Having noticed her emotion, her husband later asked about the conversation. When she explained that they had been discussing her relationship with Jesus, he angrily objected, "That's none of his business!" "Oh," she replied, "but, it *is* his business!" The woman had sensed the genuineness of the man's compassionate witness. The more you genuinely care about people, the more freedom they will give you to share the Gospel.

. . . Not As Dollar Signs

Some view people as dollars to be gained. When I was a student at Baylor University, I met another student who was working his way through college by selling insurance. One day over a cup of coffee, he remarked, "Every person I meet means five dollars to me." He had calculated how many people he had to contact to make a sale. He had averaged his income per sale and concluded that every person he met was worth five dollars to him. Immediately, a red flag went up in my mind. *And I wonder just how much I mean to you!*

I found out—about five dollars! The student's lack of ethical integrity soon became apparent when he attempted to use our relationship to support his dishonest behavior.

God forbid that such an attitude should become the motivation for a Christian. Yet it's possible. A church leader, in discussing the budget of his church, was heard to say, "We need to get out and reach more people. We've got a building debt to pay off!"

Seeing people as dollars to be gained may lead churches

and members to forsake evangelism. Rather than reaching out to unbelievers in the name of Christ, discipling, and equipping them, we may focus on attempting to gather into our church's membership those who are already Christians and who will be more likely to give to the budget. Such an attitude becomes a barrier to the work of the Holy Spirit in empowering Christians to reach the lost.

. . . Not As Numbers

Some see people as numbers to be counted. Do not misunderstand. Numbers—representing people—are important. The Bible makes much of numbers. They can be exciting and motivating. Yet the Good Shepherd in Jesus' story left the ninety-nine safe in the fold and went in search of the one lost sheep. Each one is important to God.

Jesus fed the *five thousand*. Peter preached at Pentecost and about *three thousand* believed and were baptized (Acts 2:41). Who counted? Why were the numbers recorded in the Word of God? Each number represents a person. Christians are encouraged by hearing the testimony of God's work in the lives of others.

Numbers, however, are not primary. *People* are primary. We must not use numbers for numbers' sake nor for the purpose of boasting. We need to see people as God's highest creation, as greatly loved and designed for His glorious purpose with great potential for His glory.

One day while I was visiting in the Chicago area, I knocked on the door of a man named Bob. In the course of our conversation, I asked, "Have you come to know Jesus Christ in a personal way, or would you say that you are still in the process?"

With deep emotion, Bob replied, "Oh, I know Him. I really do!"

"Please, tell me how it happened," I asked.

Bob told me his story. "For twenty years, I was a wino on

the streets of Chicago. One cold, wintry day, with newspapers stuffed in my coat for warmth and cardboard in my shoes, I wandered into a mission center to get a bowl of soup. I heard them tell about Jesus. A few days later, I went to another mission for soup. They, too, shared about Jesus. I went away different, with a new warmth inside. I got a little job. I bought some clothes and got a room. Later, I got a better job. I sought and found my wife. She had been waiting for twenty years. We got back together. Jesus changed my life and gave me back my home!"

"That's marvelous, Bob," I said, rejoicing with him. "May I ask you another question? Have you confessed Christ and become a part of a church fellowship?"

"No, do I need to do that?"

"Yes, you do." I had the privilege of showing him from God's Word how important it was to publicly confess Christ and be a part of a local body of believers. Bob indicated that he was ready to do exactly what Jesus would have him do. He soon joined a local church.

Bob is more that just a number. He is God's creation with wonderful potential for Christ. He needed the life-changing Gospel of Christ. He could have been considered as just an insignificant number, just another homeless drunk on the street. But someone—Bob did not even remember who—served him a bowl of soup and shared Jesus with him. With God, everybody is somebody. In Christ there is hope for the Bobs we pass on the street. He cares about every single one and wants to use us to reach out to them with the Gospel.

People are not objects to be manipulated, dollars to be gained, or numbers to be counted. They are precious to God and should be to us. Every time I meet a street person, or walk around a wino lying on the street, or encounter someone trapped in seeming hopeless bondage to sin, I think of Bob, because with God, there are no hopeless cases. Bob's story shows that, with God, there is unlimited potential for those we might consider hopeless.

... *But As Individuals Jesus Loves*

I love the story of Jesus and His compassion as He cleansed the leper: "And Jesus, moved with compassion, put out His hand and touched him, and said to him, 'I am willing; be cleansed'" (Mark 1:41 NKJV). Jesus could have zapped the leper from a distance with healing power. The filthy leper, with the odor of decaying flesh, probably had not felt a human touch in years. In fact, he was forced by law to ring a bell and shout, "Unclean, unclean!" to warn people of his approach. He was not permitted to come within twenty feet of another person. But Jesus put forth His hand and *touched* him. The touch of compassion is the touch of the Christian witness. People need a loving touch. They need your touch and mine as we share Jesus with them. They need the touch of Jesus through our sharing His Gospel and through the ministry of the Holy Spirit.

So Listen to People

Effective listening is the key to communication. The person-centered witness seeks not only to understand the words, but to hear the hearts of others. A barrage of words, however true and meaningful, may cause the person to clam up and not hear anything at all. To receive the words of witness, a person must be open to consider what is said.

Listening helps a person feel accepted enough to become open in the witnessing conversation. It says, "I care." Multitudes of hurting people yearn for someone to care enough to listen. It allows them to unburden their hearts and share where they really are spiritually. Listening establishes a rapport that breaks down barriers. Many need to be listened to more than to be preached at.

Dr. John Drakeford, in his book *The Awesome Power of the Listening Ear*, told a delightful story.[†] While serving as interim pastor of a church, he observed Jean, a young single woman, who was always surrounded by a group of friends. Jean was always accompanied by an escort—usually someone different each time—at the various church functions. She brought many guests to Sunday school and church with her. Though not particularly beautiful, Jean attracted people to her in an unusual way.

Dr. Drakeford decided to get to know her to discover the reason for her excellent rapport with people and asked her to meet him in the pastor's office for an interview. "Jean, tell me about yourself. I've noticed that you have many friends."

"Oh, Dr. Drakeford," the young woman replied, "I've never accomplished much, but you're such a marvelous person. You're from Australia, a great teacher and preacher, and a world traveler. I'd really like to hear more about _you_."

Dr. Drakeford began to talk, while Jean listened intently, wide-eyed, hanging onto every word. "I talked about myself," he said, "oblivious to what was happening until suddenly I realized why so many were attracted to her. She listened to people!"

Indeed, there is awesome power in the listening ear. You can almost listen some people into the kingdom of God as you guide the conversation and share Jesus with them.

Active listening will help you understand people and be able to discern at what point you can meaningfully share Christ and His way of salvation. Listening will help you draw the other person out. It will enable people to talk about themselves, their joys, needs, and problems. As an effective listener, you can use basic counseling techniques.

- Always exhibit courtesy and interest.

- Give your full attention to the person.

- Use restatements of what the person has said.

For example, Jean might have said, "I grew up never feeling loved. I am the middle child in a family of three children."

You may use restatement by saying, "Oh, you never felt loved."

This procedure is a nonthreatening method of giving an opportunity to deal with the painful experience of feeling unloved.

Remember, this is little more than a technique or a come-on if not combined with genuine love for the person who is speaking. I remember speaking with a man who said with great emotion that he had no use for the church. There was obviously pain behind that statement, and because I cared for him, I wanted to know more. As we continued to share, I remarked, "You said you have no use for the church. Can you tell me about that?" Sensing that I would not condemn him for his feelings, he began to pour out his earlier disappointments with the church, revealing his bitterness. For some time he had felt that the church did not care about him. As he vented his emotions, he began to feel that someone from the church did care. His attitude began to change. He not only became open to Christ, he trusted Him as Lord and Savior. This man who had no use for the church became an active member, living for Christ.

Ask nonthreatening questions. Then, if there is no immediate response from the listener, use silence. Often a person is silent because he is thinking about how to say what is on his heart. Or, she may be struggling with a deep emotion. If the witness is uncomfortable with silence and begins to talk, the person may never surface the issue with which she is struggling. Silence often allows the other person freedom to become open without becoming defensive. Pauses in conversation can be effective.

In person-centered witnessing, listening often will open

the door for presentation of the Gospel. Each person is like an island. If you are in a boat, you may have to circle the island to find a port of entry. Then you can know the best point for landing.

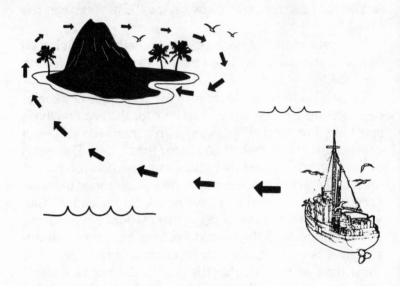

So Love People

The chief ingredient in effectively sharing Jesus is love. It's not only *like* God, the Scripture declares that "God is love" (1 John 4:8). The Greek word used in the New Testament for the God kind of love is *agape*. *Agape* love is unconditional. It does not say, "I love you if . . ." or "I love you because . . . ." It says, "I love you in spite of . . . , regardless of . . . , and no matter what!"

Love is not permissive. Holy God hates sin. It is foreign to His very nature and destructive to His creation. His judgment is against all sin. However, God loves every person in spite of sin. His love distinguishes between the sin and the sinner. God so loved us that in spite of our sins,

He gave His highest and best for us—His Son (John 3:16). This kind of love is from God. It comes from within and is not dependent on the object of our love. There is nothing a person can do to keep the Christian from loving him or her. Love does not condemn. It is not selective.

Love overcomes the *barriers* we face in sharing Jesus. Such love comes from an abiding experience with God as Christ lives within us and fills our lives. First Corinthians 13 describes this love as patient, kind, never envying, not boastful, not proud, not rude, not self-seeking, not easily angered, keeping no record of wrongs, not delighting in evil, rejoicing in truth, protecting, trusting, hoping, persevering, and never failing.

The first characteristic of love listed in 1 Corinthians 13 is patience. Love endures anything to reach the person. It is persistent, overlooks slights, and never becomes discouraged. It keeps at the task. It does not take personally the attitudes, actions, and behavior of other people.

A humorous illustration comes from the business world. A relatively new and discouraged insurance salesperson turned in his briefcase. "I've been insulted for the last time," he complained.

A veteran salesperson, overhearing, said, "I don't understand. I've had doors slammed in my face, been pushed down stairs, had dogs sicced on me. But insulted? Never!"

God's love filling you and me will give us the ability to keep on in spite of the negative responses we face as we share Jesus. Like the mature salesperson, we will not take personally the responses of others to the Gospel we share. Discouragement is one of the barriers that keeps us from sharing Jesus. Apart from God's love it would paralyze us. Fear is another powerful barrier to consistent Christian witness. But love cancels fear. "There is no fear in love. But perfect love drives out fear" (1 John 4:18 NIV). You can overcome fear through the maturing of God's love within your own life. If He lives in us, we become capable of real love for others, and His love flows through us to them. "If anyone acknowledges that Jesus is the Son of God, God lives in him and he in God. And so we know and rely on the love God has for us. God is love. Whoever lives in love lives in God, and God in him. Love is made complete among us so that we will have confidence on the day of judgment, because in this world we are like him" (vv. 15–17).

Fear says, "How will I be received? I may not know what to say. I may make a mistake. I may drive them away. I may foul up." The one word used most in these fear-rooted statements is "I." Fear is centered in self. In fact, it is no exaggeration to say that pride is at the root of fear. There is no fear in love. You are not afraid of a person you love. When you love Jesus and people, you will do your best to lead them to Him.

"I don't want to get involved with people anymore. Every time I do, I get hurt," some will say. Indeed, involvement with people sometimes brings pain, but who do we think we are to be exempt from pain? The Lord we profess to follow became totally involved with people to the extent that it killed Him! The servant is not greater than his Master. If we follow Him, we will risk being hurt to share Him and glorify Him.

Never forget that those without Christ are in a desperate situation, regardless of how comfortable or prosperous they may appear on the outside. People usually can't extricate themselves from desperate situations. They need help. They need someone to intervene. Without the loving intervention of someone, the situation is unlikely to change.

Intervention is necessary to reach others for Christ. Unless a Christian cares enough to take a chance in sharing the Gospel of Christ, the lost will likely die without hope, separated from God. There is always risk involved when you share Jesus. But agape love and trust in the Holy Spirit will enable the Christian to exercise the intervention of personal witnessing.

I'll never forget what an emergency nurse told me one day: "I want to thank you for teaching me how to share Jesus. Reaching those who don't know Christ reminds me of doing CPR in the emergency room. My ER training tells me that when they bring in a patient who's not breathing and whose heart isn't beating, *Do something!* Even if you don't know what to do. Do something! If you don't, they're gone."

Even when we're not sure of what to do, we must trust the Holy Spirit and love enough to intervene. Sharing Christ is vital to those around us.

† John W. Drakeford, *The Awesome Power of the Listening Heart*, (Grand Rapids, MI, Zondervan, 1982).

Chapter Five: Personal Review Questions

1. What are some of the warning signs that we are not really seeing the people we come face to face with every day?

2. What are the conditions in our culture which make it difficult to really see the people we come face to face with every day?

3. What adjustments need to be made in priorities or schedule which will help us to see the people around us every day?

4. What motive would cause Christians to stop their busy schedules long enough to recognize someone they hardly know and listen to them in a way that shows they really care?

5. What does it mean to love someone for Iesus' sake?

6. What does that kind of love look like?

Chapter 6

You Share Jesus with People Who Act Like They Act Because They Are Where They Are!

Lost! The tragedy of lostness is heartbreaking. The Greek word for "lost" means "to perish, to experience wasted existence in this life and in eternity, to be utterly destroyed."[†]

Sensitivity to lostness is *extremely* important to sharing Christ meaningfully. Realizing the consequences of being lost on the mental, emotional, and spiritual lives of people will help prepare you to relate meaningfully to them where they are.

Remember What It Means to Be Lost

Why should a Christian consider what it means to be lost? The Bible focuses on the lost condition of those without Christ. Over and over in the Scriptures, God surfaces different aspects of lostness. Realizing what it means to be lost will intensify our concern and reinforce our urgency in witnessing.

The report that someone has been diagnosed with AIDS intensifies our concern for that person. We know what AIDS does to a person. Lostness is the AIDS of the soul.

Unlike AIDS, for which there *is* no known cure, there is a cure for lostness—but only *one*. And that cure is Jesus, who is the way, the truth, and the life (John 14:6).

To withhold knowledge of the cure for any awful disease for any reason whatsoever is unthinkable. Who could be so caught up in the depths of selfishness? Who could be so unloving?

No wonder that when we get our eyes off ourselves and focus on the spiritual condition of unbelievers before God we banish selfish inhibitions and tell the world about the cure Christ brings.

The love of Christ compels us to share the news naturally with no thought of how it will affect us. We have great news for the world! After all, that's what the word *Gospel* means—good news!

Remember to Be Sensitive to the Lost

Many Christians have all but forgotten what it is like to be without Christ. It doesn't take long to forget. Once a person comes into the light and liberty of Christ, the memory of living in the darkness and bondage of sin soon becomes a dim, distant memory.

Jerry was a young crop duster pilot who had never found Christ as his Savior. His wife was an active church member who loved to sing in the choir. I shared the Gospel with Jerry several times, but each time he courteously but firmly turned down the invitation to come to Christ.

Jerry loved auto racing and often drove his own car in the Sunday races. But one Easter Sunday, he was in church. He heard the message of the cross and resurrection of Christ.

On Wednesday night after prayer meeting, the Lord impressed upon me that I should see Jerry right away. I grabbed a doctor friend and went over to his house.

"I'm glad to see you. I've been thinking about the message of Easter I heard last Sunday." Then he began to rehearse the story of Jesus going to the cross and rising again.

I interrupted, "Jerry, that's why we're here. We came to ask you to trust Christ."

Jerry called his wife out of the kitchen, "Come in here, honey! I'm going to become a Christian tonight!"

As we prayed, Jerry poured out his heart to God. He asked Jesus to forgive his sins and come into his heart. The Holy Spirit had done His convicting work. An enthusiastic Jerry jumped up from his knees and said, "Pastor, what can I do now for Jesus?"

"Jerry," I said, "you have a friend named Johnny who doesn't know Christ. He's in about the same situation you were in. Tomorrow night you can go tell Johnny what has happened to you. Doc will go with you, won't you, Doc?"

"I surely will!" the doctor declared joyfully.

The next Sunday both Jerry and Johnny were in church, where they made public their decision to follow Christ as Lord and Savior. They were joined by the doctor and their wives. It was a holy moment!

The next week Jerry came to see me early in the morning. Something bothered him. "I've been sharing about Jesus with my friend Sammy. But he's not interested. I just can't understand it! How can he act like that?"

Although Jerry had only been a Christian for one week, he had already forgotten what it was like to be lost. It doesn't take long to forget!

Remember the Consequences of Being Lost

The Scriptures are clear in speaking about the condition of the lost. Numerous passages from the Bible describe lostness.

Lost: Under Sin

The lost are trapped under sin, living in a state of spiritual gloom, blocked from experiencing the "light" of the Son. "What shall we conclude then? Are we any better? Not at all! We have already made the charge that Jews and Gentiles are all under sin" (Rom. 3:9 NIV). God is holy and is above sin. Humanity is sinful and is under sin. "All have sinned and fall short of the glory of God" (v. 23). Between holy God and sinful humanity there is an impenetrable sin barrier that separates the human race from God.

When we were without Christ, we were under sin's power. The heartbreaking result of being under sin is expressed in Romans 3:10–18: "'There is no one righteous, not even one; / there is no one who understands, / no one who seeks God. / All have turned away, they have together become worthless; / there is no one who does good, not even one.' / 'Their throats are open graves; their tongues practice deceit.' / 'The poison of vipers is on their lips.' / 'Their mouths are full of cursing and bitterness.' / 'Their feet are swift to shed blood; ruin and misery mark their ways, / and the way of peace they do not know.' / 'There is no fear of God before their eyes'" (NIV).

The human race is universally religious. Within each life is an insatiable yearning for God. The vacuum within drives people to attempt to satisfy their hearts' need. Human pride causes the search for satisfaction and meaning to be done independently of God. Through self-effort, good works, and religious performance, they strive to justify themselves and reach God in their own way. *But none can penetrate the sin barrier.* Human effort can never be strong enough or effective enough to eradicate sin and reach God. Through the prophet Isaiah, God revealed: "As the heavens are higher than the earth, / so are my ways higher than your ways / and my thoughts than your thoughts" (55:9 NIV).

Sin has so *infected* and *affected* everyone that each possesses an inherent tendency toward evil. The natural bent toward sin results in attitudes and acts of disobedience to God. Sin is a disease of the character that humans *cannot cure*. It is a flaw in personality that humans *cannot correct*.

This does not mean that we are all immoral criminals and traitors. Nor does it mean that we always do evil and perverted things. It does mean that God is perfect and holy. His standard for us is His perfection and holiness. We are incapable of measuring up to God's standard.

The first man, Adam, introduced sin into the world. This resulted in separation from God, and death—not just for Adam but for each of us. And we can't point a finger of blame at Adam to attempt to escape personal responsibility and guilt, for Romans 5:12 answers the question of account-ability: "Therefore, just as sin entered the world through one man, and death through sin, and in this way death came to all men, because all sinned" (NIV). All of us have sinned by our own choice and so are responsible. None of us have any basis for arguing that we are not responsible for our coming short of God's plan for us. "So that every mouth may be silenced and the whole world held accountable to God" (3:19 NIV). We are responsible for our own sin.

Like leaden clouds covering the earth on a cold February day, so the barrier of sin places unbelievers under an emo-tional and spiritual cloud of gloom. It permeates life with dread and desperation. In an effort to cope or escape, many try to ignore or deny the reality of their state by filling their lives with hyperactivity or absorbing themselves with pleasure. Some drive themselves to achieve, trying to dem-onstrate their own worth and silence the void within them that calls out to God.

If only we, like Jesus, could see lost, hurting people *as* they really are and *where* they really are—then we, too, would be moved with compassion for them. The whole realm of existence for people without Jesus should stimu-late us to prayer and urgency in sharing the Good News.

The *only* hope for their salvation is God's intervention. He did what no other could ever do. God Himself penetrated the sin barrier by coming in and through the person of Jesus Christ. Jesus came into our situation to live a sinless life, to bear the sin of the world on the cross, and to rise again. Jesus broke through the sin barrier to provide the way for us to come to God through Him. It happened in my life, and it can happen in yours and in all who will receive Him. At that moment, He brings us through the sin barrier into a new relationship with the Father. Through Christ, we become His new creation, living in a righteous relationship with God. Sin has no more authority over our lives.

Lost: Spiritually Dead

Without Christ, the lost are spiritually dead. They are physically, mentally, and emotionally alive, but spiritually dead. This means they are separated from God and have no spiritual life with Him. "For the wages of sin is death" (Rom. 6:23 NIV). "As for you, you were dead in your transgressions and sins, in which you used to live when you followed the ways of this world and of the ruler of the kingdom of the air, the spirit who is now at work in those who are disobedient" (Eph. 2:1–2 NIV).

John was a successful business executive. However, his success did not bring the satisfaction he had anticipated through years of driving himself. He had felt that reaching his goals of achieving position and affluence would make him happy. But it had come to the point that no matter what he achieved, there was no real and permanent satisfaction. He struggled with a lack of inner peace and purpose.

"I just feel dead inside," he said.

It is a great tragedy for a man to work hard all his life but fail to reach his goals; it's an even greater tragedy for a man to work hard and to reach his goals only to find them empty.

A Christian friend noticed John's angst and need. He told John about his own experience, about how coming to know Christ makes so much difference. John's friend used familiar Bible passages in witnessing (see Chapter 11).

John realized that he felt dead because he was dead! Dead in trespasses and sin. Spiritually dead. He'd been existing, not living. He needed real life.

You know, an egg is alive—almost. Actually it's only potentially alive.

An egg gets born once to be a potential living chick, but if that egg is not hatched—born a second time—it will degenerate in its own shell.

When John's friend led him to Christ, the executive came to life and broke out of his shell, so to speak, to live God's way; he was born again. Whereas before John had just been existing, he really came to life through faith in Jesus Christ. He found true success which his position and possessions had not been able to bring.

In the Garden of Eden, God commanded Adam not to eat of the fruit of the tree of knowledge of good and evil. "For when you eat of it," God said, "you will surely die" (Gen. 2:17 NIV). Adam rebelled against God's command and ate the forbidden fruit. He did not die immediately, however, though the process of physical death was set in motion. But separated from God, he did die spiritually. Intimacy in relationship and fellowship with the Creator who loved him was gone.

Spiritual deadness permeates the entire being of people who don't know Christ. It affects everything they do. They have no intimacy or communion with God. There can be no spiritual relationship with those who know the Lord. Spiritual deadness takes its toll on the body, mind, and emotion; life is lived in sorrowful aloneness. Only one breath, one heartbeat stands between unbelievers and eternal death and separation from God in hell.

The spiritually dead cannot bring themselves to life, no

matter how sincerely and ardently they try. They must be given life through the life-generating Holy Spirit as they are born again by faith in Jesus Christ. Nicodemus was religious, respectable, rich—a respected ruler—but he was spiritually dead! He betrayed the reality of his inner dissatisfaction and turmoil by coming for a nighttime interview with Jesus. Jesus got directly to the point of his need when He said, "I tell you the truth, unless a man is born again, he cannot see the kingdom of God" (John 3:3 NIV). The only hope for spiritual and eternal life is the new birth through Christ.

Lost: Children of Wrath

People without Christ live under the abiding cloud of God's wrath. "Among these we as well as you once lived and conducted ourselves in the passions of our flesh—our behavior governed by our corrupt and sensual nature; obeying the impulses of the flesh and the thoughts of the mind—our cravings dictated by our senses and our dark imaginings. We were then by nature children of [God's] wrath and heirs of [His] indignation, like the rest of mankind" (Eph. 2:3 AMPLIFIED BIBLE). His impending judgment on sin is an ever-present threat to the sinner (John 3:36). "But because of your stubbornness and your unrepentant heart, you are storing up wrath against yourself for the day of God's wrath, when his righteous judgment will be revealed. God 'will give to each person according to what he has done'" (Rom. 2:5–6 NIV).

The river of God's wrath is being held back like a mighty reservoir behind a dam. When the dam breaks, the flood of God's anger against sin will overflow to sweep the lost to destruction. As objects of wrath, unbelievers live in a continuous state of peril. Sensing their peril, they experience the constant yet often unconscious anxiety anticipating judgment.

The gravity of the human situation led Jesus to give three illustrations of lostness from the perspective of the loser:

The lost sheep was in grave danger and peril (Luke 15:3–7). The shepherd left ninety-nine sheep in safety to go in search of the one lost sheep. And when the sheep was found, he called all his friends and neighbors to rejoice with him. Jesus indicated that heaven rejoices when one sinner repents.

The lost coin was of such value to the woman who owned it that she swept her house and searched until she found it. Then she called her friends and neighbors to help her celebrate (vv. 8–10).

The younger son left his home to go seek his fortune in a far country. There, separated from his father, he fell into sin. The father watched and waited, longing for his return. When the son came home, the father threw a homecoming party (vv. 11–32).

In the three stories, Jesus taught the value of one individual and illustrated the sorrowful state of the lost. That condition is one of danger and peril, uselessness, wasted existence, sinfulness, depravity, and separation from the Father.

Lost: Separated from Christ

"Remember that at that time you were separate from Christ" (Eph. 2:12 NIV). Can you imagine what it would be like to be without Christ and to have no possibility of forgiveness for sin? Forgiveness through Christ is the only way to have a pure conscience before God. What if the guilt of sin still weighed heavily upon your mind and heart? When the lost lay their heads on their pillows at night, their guilt is before them. When they awaken, they cannot escape. People drink barrels of alcohol and take bushels of pills in the attempt to ease the pain and guilt of their sin. Many attempt to cope with sin through counseling. In desperation, some even decide to end it all in suicide. Still others try to "tough it out," attempting to convince themselves that they can carry the heavy load of their unforgiven sin.

It is no wonder the lost act like they do! They are lost! But when Jesus comes into a life, the person's sins are forgiven. There is release from guilt, cleansing from sin, and power through the Spirit to live for Christ.

Lost: Without God

Unbelievers are "without God in the world" (Eph. 2:12 NIV). They may acknowledge His existence. They may even attempt to live by His moral law. They may be law-abiding citizens and do good works. Out of His mercy and love, God blesses them with life and provides for them. "He causes his sun to rise on the evil and the good, and sends rain on the righteous and the unrighteous" (Matt. 5:45 NIV). While God is very near to unbelievers, they do not know Him. They feel far from Him.

How long has it been since you reflected upon how people without Jesus feel and what they face? How miserable it would be to live outside the purpose of the One who made us; what unspeakable sorrow to live in rebellion against God who loves us so much that He gave His Son for us. It is no wonder Jesus wept openly as He stood on the Mount of Olives and looked across the city filled with so many lost, hurting people.

Lost: Without Hope

"Excluded from citizenship in Israel and foreigners to the covenants of promise, without hope" (Eph. 2:12 NIV). The most pitiful state of existence is to be without hope. We can endure unimaginable difficulty and suffering as long as we have hope that one day we will come through it.

Betty, a forty-one-year-old mother of five, took her own life after leaving her husband and family for another man and discovering that she was pregnant with his baby. "Hell could be no worse than this," she wrote in her suicide note. Betty was tragically mistaken. In hell, the hopelessness is forever and forever. Milton has this sign at the portal of hell: "Abandon hope, all ye who enter here."

Of all the horrors of hell, hopelessness is the worst. Jesus spoke about the hopelessness of hell in Luke 16:26: "And besides all this, between us and you a great chasm has been fixed, so that those who want to go from here to you cannot, nor can anyone cross over from there to us" (NIV). If a person could be in hell for a thousand or a million years and have a ray of hope of ever escaping, it would not be hell. Make no mistake, hell is a place of unbearable, inescapable, and unending suffering and sorrow for those who live and die without Christ.

In this life and in eternity, Jesus is our only hope. None of us have any ability in ourselves to undo our sin and escape hell. Because of our sin, all of us deserve hell. But because of His grace, those who have trusted Christ become forgiven children of God, with a home in heaven. Those who reject Christ are living in this world without hope and face eternity without hope.

Lost: Condemned Already

"Whoever believes in him is not condemned, but whoever does not believe stands condemned already because he has not believed in the name of God's one and only Son" (John 3:18 NIV). The Greek root word for "condemned" means "to judge, to give sentence, to undergo the process of a trial"[††]. Unbelievers have already been judged and found guilty. At the cross, the sin of humanity was judged.

But Christ bore the judgment for all who believe in Him. But unbelievers, because they reject Christ, *face all the consequences of sin themselves*. They are under the sentence of condemnation. Their pardon has been purchased by the shed blood of Jesus, the Lamb of God, of course. But as long as they continue in unbelief, their condemnation is certain. The moment death comes to someone apart from Christ, they will be in hell. Consequently, those who don't know Christ often choose to deliberately ignore or forget God's warnings concerning their condition and its consequences (2 Peter 3:3–10).

The other side of the coin covers the believer (v. 18). When a person by simple faith comes to Christ, the condemnation is lifted. Dread is replaced by confidence in the face of judgment for those who trust Him.

Lost: Against Jesus

"He who is not with me is against me" (Matt. 12:30 NIV). Many claim that they are for Jesus, but do not follow or obey Him. Some *say* they love Jesus and believe in Him, but do not trust Him as Savior and Lord; their declaration is empty.

In relationship to Jesus, there is no neutral ground. There are no neutral people. Our Lord indicated that if people are not trusting Him, they are against Him. Those who have a positive emotion for Jesus but no saving faith have no knowledge of true salvation. "Then Jesus said to his disciples, 'If anyone would come after me, he must deny himself and take up his cross and follow me. For whoever wants to save his life will lose it, but whoever loses his life for me will find it'" (Matt. 16:24–25 NIV).

Lost: In Sin

"I told you that you would die in your sins; if you do not believe that I am the one I claim to be, you will indeed die in your sins" (John 8:24 NIV). Romans 3:23 declares, "For all have sinned and fall short of the glory of God" (NIV). The Bible defined sin as "missing the mark." It is a word picture of an archer who aims at a target representing God's will, character, and glory. The arrow falls short—misses the mark—of the glory of God. The expression of sin within a life is transgression of the law of God (James 2:9–11; 1 John 3:4) and disobedience.

Sin is described by such words as *iniquity, wickedness, lawlessness, vile affections, offense,* and *crookedness*. Refusing to believe that Jesus is who He claims to be and to receive Him as Savior and Lord is the sin that condemns. Unredeemed people live in the realm of sin. Their position is one of crookedness, twistedness, and failure. Jesus is not in their lives.

Lost: Children of the Devil

"You belong to your father, the devil, and you want to carry out your father's desire" (John 8:44 NIV). The severity of these words of Jesus is shocking. They were spoken by our Lord to people who were respectable—even religious—but who had rejected Him. Most unbelievers aren't aware that they belong to the devil. However, their lives are directed by his purposes because they reject Christ. Without knowing it, they have allowed their lives to fit hand in glove into the devil's strategy. Like their father, the devil, they choose the self-centered life of going their own way, living independently of God.

But when someone trusts Christ, God births the person into His family to be His child to live in fellowship with

Him. As a child of the Father, the desire to please Him and serve Him characterizes life.

Lost: Enemies of God

"For if, when we were God's enemies, we were reconciled to him through the death of his Son, how much more, having been reconciled, shall we be saved through his life!" (Rom. 5:10 NIV). As enemies, the lost strive against God and His will and plan for their lives. The spiritual war is often unconscious, but nonetheless real. Among other things, it manifests itself in resistance to the Gospel as it is shared. But friendship with God happens as a person trusts Christ. Instead of striving against Him, the believer begins to seek to live by God's will and plan.

Lost: No Peace

"And the way of peace they do not know" (Rom. 3:17 NIV). "But the wicked are like the tossing sea, which cannot rest, whose waves cast up mire and mud. / 'There is no peace,' says my God, 'for the wicked'" (Isa. 57:20–21 NIV).

The first time I saw the churning waves of the Pacific Ocean, I recalled these verses and my own lack of peace before I knew Christ as my Redeemer. The tossing of the sea triggered memories of unbelieving friends and brought tears to my eyes. They had no peace. They were enduring constant turmoil and restlessness. Like the sea, the waters of their lives churned up to the surface evidence of their own depravity.

Many unbelievers become subject to deceptions that offer peace but in reality give no peace. Driven by their yearning for inner assurance, they may even fall under the spell of authoritarian cultist leaders.

This kind of inner turmoil and isolation made Victor and his wife prime targets for the cultic group that came to their door. Feeling the need for friends and someone to give them direction and support, the couple joined the cult and advanced to leadership positions.

Their inner restlessness persisted. The cult used the family's insecurity to control their lives; Victor and his wife tried to resolve their lack of peace with more aggressive cultic activities; and the cycle continued for several years. Eventually, Victor became ill and was diagnosed as having leukemia. Knowing that his illness was terminal, he was thoroughly shaken.

Their insurance agent, who was a committed Christian, began to minister to Victor and his wife. Gently he began to share Jesus with them as he had opportunity and introduced them to other Christians from his church. Within a few weeks, Victor and his wife committed their lives to Christ. "I've never known such love and peace in all my life," Victor said. And in the two years before his death, he became a vibrant witness and shared Jesus with others.

Some people manifest their inner turmoil by focusing on pleasure, position, prosperity, and power. They hope to satisfy their longing for peace by filling their lives with the earthly, the sensual, and the temporal. Others retreat into isolation, inactivity, and indifference for self-protection. But they are all longing for that which can be found only in Jesus. "Therefore, since we have been justified through faith, we have peace with God through our Lord Jesus Christ" (Rom. 5:1 NIV).

Lost: Spiritually Blind

"And even if our gospel is veiled, it is veiled to those who are perishing. The god of this age has blinded the minds of unbelievers, so that they cannot see the light of the gospel of the glory of Christ, who is the image of God" (2 Cor. 4:3–4 NIV). The beauty of God's world means nothing to those who cannot see. The light of Christ is glorious, but the lost are blinded by sin and cannot behold His majesty. The Gospel is hidden from them.

Imagine that you are in a large facility with no windows and no exterior source of light. The building is filled with people. A tornado strikes and the lights go out. The people panic. They stumble over chairs and fall down steps. They trample one another. They are in darkness. They cannot see how to move about nor find a door. Unbelievers are like blind people feeling for a wall. They wander aimlessly, stumbling to destruction.

When the light comes on, the people can see clearly how to walk directly to the door. They see people and objects so they can walk a straight path.

Unbelievers' minds cannot comprehend the reality and truth of God. The Holy Spirit must enlighten their minds as the Gospel is shared with them. "The man without the Spirit does not accept the things that come from the Spirit of God, for they are foolishness to him, and he cannot understand them, because they are spiritually discerned" (1 Cor. 2:14 NIV).

When someone looks to Christ and trusts Him, the Holy Spirit reveals the things of God to that mind and heart. He becomes a new believer and begins to grow in Christ.

Remember That the Lost Will Act Lost

"Why do lost people act like they act?" is the question many Christians ask. Witnesses for Christ sometimes have difficulty realizing why the lost resist the Gospel and react negatively. Lack of understanding of the condition and responses of unbelievers silences the witness of many Christians.

Let me say it again: People act like they act because they

are where they are. They behave as they do as a result of their spiritual condition. Don't be surprised or shocked when unbelievers act lost. They *are* lost. Sinful attitudes and actions characterize those who don't know Christ.

†Gerhard Kittle; *Theological Dictionary of the New Testament* (Wm. B. Erdmans Publishing Co., Grand Rapids, MI) 1977, 394–396.

††W.E. Vine, *Expository Dictionary of New Testament Words* (MacDonald Publishing Co., McLean, VA) 619–620.

Chapter Six: Personal Review Questions

1. What are the similarities and differences between being physically lost and spiritually lost?

2. How would you describe the concept of spiritual lostness to an adult? To a child?

3. How does the Scripture define the condition of being lost? What other terms does the Scripture use for a person who does not know Jesus?

Chapter 7

You Share Jesus with People Starting Where They Are

"Ya gotta start with 'em where they are to make good football players out of these kids!" the high school coach said in an interview with the local paper.

The coach's statement is equally true in reaching people for Jesus. You have to start with people where they are or you will seldom get through to them with the Gospel. The catch is that they are at varying levels of spiritual understanding and development.

When Linda told her new neighbor, "Jesus loves you," the surprising response was, "Jesus? Who is that?"

It is amazing that there are many in America who have never heard of Jesus. Some—refugees, immigrants, and temporary residents—have recently arrived in our country. The foreign mission field has come to us. And it's not just new immigrants who have never heard; others who have never heard are lifelong residents of our communities.

A poll conducted by George Gallup revealed that eight out of ten adult Americans claim that they believe the Bible is the revealed Word of God; however, only 35 percent of those surveyed could name all four Gospels!

And while a whopping 86 percent of the people surveyed agreed that the Ten Commandments are valid, only 40 percent of the Protestants could name even five of them.

We can't assume that unbelievers know anything at all about the Gospel. We must spell it out for them.

The apostle Paul was one of the most effective people the world has known in sharing Jesus. He sought to truly understand the people God called him to. Wisely, he tailored his approach to the individual characteristics, culture, and background of the person with whom he was sharing. He revealed his strategy clearly when he said,

> Though I am free and belong to no man, I make myself a slave to everyone, to win as many as possible. To the Jews, I became like a Jew, to win the Jews. To those under the law I became like one under the law (though I myself am not under the law), so as to win those under the law. To those not having the law I became like one not having the law (though I am not free from God's law but am under Christ's law), so as to win those not having the law. To the weak I became weak, to win the weak. I have become all things to all men so that by all possible means I might save some. I do all this for the sake of the gospel, that I may share in its blessings. (1 Cor. 9:19–23 NIV)

Paul shared essentially the same message of Christ with all the different people he met. And how could he have done differently? The Gospel message is as simple as it is unchanging. Every one of us has one problem: we've "missed the mark." And for this there is one solution: the good news of forgiveness through faith in Jesus. But Paul varied his approach *according to the need of the individual.* To the people in Athens he declared that the true God was the one to whom they had designated an altar: "To The Unknown God." He dialogued in the marketplace with the people of Ephesus, then went from house to house, sharing the message of Jesus. He confronted the licentious Corinthians, sharing the Gospel simply and directly.

Beginning where the person is spiritually is crucial

to effective communication of the Gospel. But the particular approach to take and what to share from the Word of God should be strongly influenced by the person's level of spiritual development and perceived need. In contrast to the message-centered approach, which treats everyone the same, person-centered sharing considers the level of spiritual development of the individual with whom you are sharing. The varying levels at which you may encounter people are numerous. Several of these are:

- The Ignorance Level
- The Indifference Level
- The Hostility Level
- The Interest Level
- The Conviction Level
- The Conversion Level
- The Growing Level
- The Spiritually Declining Level

Level of Spiritual Development	Characteristic	Witnessing Tactic
Ignorance	Uninformed	Pray, instruct, nurture
Indifference	Unconcerned	Share. Confront with the claims of Christ. Ask the Holy Spirit to stir.
Hostility	Bitter, angry	Love, listen, share Jesus. Continue with patience.
Interest	Concerned	Explain the Gospel. Trust the Holy Spirit to bring conviction. Ask the person to commit to Christ.
Conviction	Heavy hearted Miserable	Call attention to work of Holy Spirit. Guide through the steps in coming to Christ. Ask the person to commit to Christ.
Conversion	Ready	Guide through the conversion experience. Instruct in how to follow Christ.
Growing	Already a Christian Following Christ	Share in fellowship. Encourage to witness. Pray together for lost acquaintances.
Spiritual Declining	Discouraged, defeated Overcome by sin	Show patience, love, listen, encourage. Help reinvolve the person in following Christ. Help bridge the gap.

The Ignorance Level

Increasingly in America, the number of people who know little or nothing about Jesus is expanding. The evangelism index based on recent surveys reveals a growing paganism in every region of our country. The population of our country is growing at a more rapid pace than the numbers of people being converted to faith in Jesus Christ. Hence, more and more of those to whom we have the opportunity to witness are at the ignorance level of spiritual understanding. They have little or no acquaintance with the Bible and its basic teachings. Some do not even know who Jesus is.

To present the plan of salvation to a person at the ignorance level would be like trying to teach an algebraic equation to a preschooler who does not yet know Arabic numerals. How do you begin to witness in such a situation? Begin where the person is. Discuss the existence of God and His creative activity. Tell how God, as an intelligent being, has communicated with the people He created. Share about humanity's original fellowship with God and our consequent separation from God. Show how God expressed His love for people by seeking out those who are lost and providing for their forgiveness (John 1:1–5, 18; 3:16).

The person at the ignorance level needs to be taught the foundational truths of the Word of God. As you do so, you will be guiding the person in discovering facts and principles that the Holy Spirit can use in developing the understanding and conviction necessary for conversion. How rapidly a person moves from spiritual ignorance to conversion depends on the work of the Holy Spirit and the receptivity of the heart.

Jane was a young woman who came from spiritual ignorance to salvation through the direction of the Holy Spirit. When she got into trouble in her hometown, in desperation her mother sent her to live with her aunt in Florida. The caring aunt brought Jane to a meeting at her church, introduced her to some people, and asked that someone visit her.

Two of the Christians she had met, Melissa and Kim, went by the furniture store where the aunt worked the very next day to see Jane. To have the opportunity for an uninterrupted conversation, they were escorted to the showroom window living room display. On the other side of that window, people were passing by on the street! But it didn't matter. The Holy Spirit can do His work in all kinds of settings.

Melissa began the conversation and was soon sharing Jesus. When she asked Jane if she would like to receive Christ as her Savior and Lord, she simply lowered her eyes and did not reply. The silence was deafening. Tension began to build.

Finally, Melissa turned to Kim and asked, "Do you have something you would like to say?"

"No. I think you've said about all that needs to be said. But I would like to ask a question."

Listening and watching, Kim had concluded that either Jane was terribly rebellious, or that she had not understood anything Melissa had said. "May I ask you a question, Jane?"

"Sure."

"Jane, I don't want to embarrass you. But please tell me some of the things you know about Jesus."

Jane seemed to be searching for an answer. Finally, hesitantly, she said, "I—I know He made light!"

Following the service the night before, she had gone home and with a seeking heart, had read from her aunt's Bible, beginning with the only place she knew to begin—the first page. Having read about creation, she recalled the creation of light! Melissa and Kim began at that point to teach and guide her in foundational understanding. Then, when they retold the good news about Jesus, Jane was ready to ask Christ into her life. This time, she prayed to receive

Christ, and the showroom window became a place of rejoicing. Jane soon began to experience a transformed life.

Discerning the spiritual level of unbelievers is crucial to effective witnessing. Those who are in spiritual ignorance need someone who will care enough to determine where they are and patiently instruct them from the Word of God.

The Indifference Level

Some people are not *ignorant* of the Gospel, they are *indifferent* to it. They know, but they do not care. Their lives are entangled with concerns that distract them from any consideration of their spiritual condition and what God has for them. Jesus spoke about these in the parable of the sower and the soils: "The seeds that fell among the thorn bushes are also people who hear the message. But they start worrying about the needs of this life and are fooled by the desire to get rich. So the message gets choked out, and they never produce anything" (Matt. 13:22).

Satan uses the cares of this world to maintain his hold on a life. He uses worldly success, failure, pleasure, money, habits, hobbies, and other things to dominate the minds of unbelievers. He uses whatever stronghold is available to keep a person from giving attention to the need of his soul.

The indifferent must be shaken out of their complacency to look to God. How can this happen? It is something we cannot do. Only God can draw people to Jesus, though He does work in and through His faithful children as His instruments to reach a spiritually starved world.

As long as the indifferent go undisturbed, however, they are likely to continue to drift. For them to consider their need of Christ, someone will have to love them enough to "rock their boat." And effective intervention begins with a burden of love for the lost. "Love covers over a multitude of sins" (1 Peter 4:8 NIV). "Remember this: Whoever turns a sinner away from his error will save him from death and cover over a multitude of sins" (James 5:20 NIV). Reaching someone for Jesus starts with caring.

Fervent prayer is also essential to reaching the indifferent. Pray for the lost person. Pray for your own spirit and attitude that you will be the sensitive witness God wants you to be. Your caring, consistent, Christ-filled life will affirm the Gospel you share. Pray for the leadership of the Holy Spirit to guide you as God works in the lost person's life. Be willing to risk, trusting God for the results by following what He leads you to do and say. Share the Good News. The Gospel has the power needed to completely blast away complacency. It pierces the heart with conviction and creates a desire for Jesus and His forgiveness.

Finally, never give up! Realize that the Holy Spirit will continue to draw to the Lord Jesus the one He has placed on your heart. Change will come. *Know that any time God places a burden for someone on your heart, the Holy Spirit is already powerfully at work in that life*. Spend time with the person and be ready to respond to the opportunity to share the Gospel.

Often, the closest Christian to the indifferent unbeliever is the primary hindrance to them trusting Christ. The inconsistent Christian life of a mate, parent, or close friend will be a difficult barrier to overcome.

This was the situation in the case of Sheri and her unbelieving husband, Dan. Sheri, who attended church spasmodically, was inconsistent in many areas of her Christian life.

One Sunday, evidently burdened by the Holy Spirit, she spoke to her pastor after church, expressing concern for her husband. "Pastor, please pray for Dan," Sheri said. "He's becoming more and more difficult to live with. He won't come to church and he doesn't want me to come. He keeps putting more and more pressure on me."

The pastor surprised himself with a spontaneous answer that was uncharacteristic of his usual responses. "Sheri, I'll pray for Dan. But, first, I'm going to pray for you. If God does a work in Dan's life, He'll have to go around you to do it."

Sheri was shaken. "Pastor, you're right," she admitted tearfully. "I'm standing in the way!"

The pastor gently asked Sheri if she would like to pray about the matter. She did so, confessing her sins to the Father and feeling His cleansing power as she yielded her life anew to Christ. At home, too, she became a different person—more considerate and loving toward her husband. As the Holy Spirit gave opportunity, she tenderly shared with her husband her concern about his spiritual condition. Within a few weeks, he was coming with her to church. Soon afterward, he received Christ. Their home became a center of redemption as they began to reach out to their neighbors and friends with the Gospel of Christ.

It does not always happen that quickly. But as those nearest the unbelieving person let Christ live His life through them, change *will* come in their relationships. The indifferent will be shaken out of their complacency. Some may begin immediately to seek the Lord. Others may gradually become open to the Word of God and to the ministry of the church. Still others may become actively rebellious. In their indifference, they have been passively rebellious against God. As the Holy Spirit convicts, however, they may actively resist God and even react with hostility toward the witness.

The Hostility Level

It is not unusual for unbelievers to move from the indifference level to the hostility level. Fear of resentful reactions tempts Christians to avoid unbelievers rather than obediently reach out with the Gospel to them. It may appear to be easier to let them go on in their desperate spiritual state rather than risk their reaction.

But when you are led to share Jesus, the Holy Spirit will stand beside you, guiding you in dealing with negative reactions. Often, unbelievers have suppressed attitudes and concepts that must be surfaced and worked through before they can come to Christ. Someone must love them with the love of Jesus enough to allow them to react defensively and yet still continue to minister to them at the point of their need, and so gently guide them to Christ.

People who are at the hostility level in their spiritual lives are angry. More than likely, their bitterness will spill over on anyone who tries to get close to them. Instead of being glad for expressions of love and concern, they will lash out in resentment. Remember, though, *people act like they act because they are where they are spiritually.* People aren't the enemy, they're the victims of the enemy!

How does one witness to hostile people? The natural tendency is to ignore them or pass them off to someone else. Another tendency is to retaliate. The attack may be in the form of condemnation, argument, or retort. But putting the person down or winning an argument will not win the person. You will only lead the lost person to the conclusion that here is another Christian who does not really care.

Person-centered sharing revolves around loving and listening. Hostile people have usually been hurt and are nursing deep disappointments. They feel that nobody loves them—not even God. They may blame Him for their troubles and refuse to consider anything the believer has to say. And when they are approached by a Christian who wants to share Jesus with them, they may instinctively react by withdrawing or by striking back.

But don't let their negativism rob you of a blessing in ministry. Listen to the person. Use the conversation guide **FIRM** (Friend, Interests, Religion, Message) to draw him or her into conversation. Depending on how quickly the Holy

Spirit leads, this may be done in one conversation or over a period of time in several conversations. Be patient. Allow the person to open up and ventilate without your becoming defensive. Set aside the time you need to establish a meaningful relationship before you attempt to share the Gospel. Loving the person is the key—not "getting a decision for Christ." Draw the person into an experience of Jesus and His love, keeping in mind that the Holy Spirit is continually working to convict and draw the person to Him.

You may not lead that person to Christ, but God may use you to help them become more open to Him. I once spent a lengthy period of time communicating with a bitter, immoral man. We became friends. I shared Jesus with him, but he would not receive Him. As I continued to share with him from time to time, others joined me in prayer and witness. Sometime later, a friend from this man's youth came through our town and visited him at his place of business. The friend, who had become a committed Christian, was able to share his testimony and lead my friend to Christ. All of us whom the Holy Spirit had used rejoiced in his salvation.

My wife and I enjoy browsing through antique stores in the areas of the country where our work takes us. While on vacation one year, we stopped by a shop and began to converse with the proprietor. When I attempted to share Jesus with him, he became furious and ordered me out of his store. I asked if I could leave him a booklet about Jesus. He threatened, shaking with anger. I did the only thing I knew to do. I left!

I drove in silence for miles, praying and trying to process all that had taken place. I was feeling hurt, disappointed, rejected. God impressed me to pray for the man and realize that the Holy Spirit was still there with the antique store owner, doing His work. This side of heaven, I may never know what happened in the man's life. But I planted a seed. Now I can trust God to bring the harvest.

The Holy Spirit is always at work, wooing the heart of the

unsaved person to Christ. He loves the angry person more than you do. He is more interested in that person's salvation than you are. It is important to remember that you are not alone in your witness. You are joining the Holy Spirit as He works.

One Saturday afternoon, Brad knocked on the door of Mr. and Mrs. King, a couple who had visited his church two Sundays before. Only last Sunday, Mrs. King had come alone and joined the church, having made her decision to follow Christ. Brad had been asked to meet with them in their home. But when he got there, he found only Mr. King.

"We're so glad you and your wife have decided to make our church your church home," Brad began after stepping inside.

Mr. King was blunt and to the point. "My wife may have decided, but I haven't decided to go to your church or any church!" And he proceeded to pour out a torrent of grievances against ministers, Christians, and the church in general.

When the man stopped for breath, Brad would insert a question that would set him off again. Mr. King was furious about churches—insisting that they were only interested in money. He knew a dishonest minister who did not pay his debts and a minister of music who had run off with the pianist. Brad listened for what seemed an eternity, refusing to become defensive or to argue with him. And when Mr. King finally ran down, Brad spoke up. "Mr. King, your wife plans to be baptized in our church. I know she would want you to be there. I'd be pleased to have you sit with me."

"What time?" Mr. King asked gruffly.

The next morning, he was present for his wife's baptism. Late the next afternoon, he phoned Brad to say that he had to talk to him, that he had not slept since their conversation on Saturday. "I can't stand it any longer," he said.

Brad was due to be in an out-of-town meeting and would not be back until about 11:00 P.M. Mr. King asked him to come by the house when he returned. And by midnight, Mr. King was pouring out his heart in repentance and receiving Christ.

What had happened? Mr. King's hostility was gone. He had ventilated his hostility on a Christian who loved him and refused to retaliate or be defensive. As soon as Mr. King had released his anger, he began to feel the emptiness of the spiritual vacuum in his life that had been there all along and the Holy Spirit was able to pierce his heart with conviction. Mr. King was free to receive the Gospel of forgiveness and became a new creation in Christ.

Many hostile people are like Mr. King. They need someone to love them as they are, to listen to them, and to share the Word of God with them as the Holy Spirit draws them to Christ.

The Interest Level

Many have heard the Gospel and are genuinely interested. They may not yet fully grasp the plan of salvation and the importance of trusting Christ. Often the interested simply need someone to guide them. They may lack the depth of conviction necessary to come with repentance to Christ.

The interested person still needs to be cultivated. He or she needs exposure to the Word of God to bring conviction. Still, it is the Holy Spirit who cultivates and convicts; we work beside Him to share the Word of God and guide the person in coming to Christ.

Those at the interest level may be ready to receive Christ as soon as the Gospel is presented. However, reaching someone for Jesus may require a longer witnessing relationship. During this time, frequent and periodic contact needs to be maintained. The ministry of a small fellowship group can be very effective in providing nurture in the Word of God and meaningful friendships with fellow group members. Sensitivity to "draw the net"—asking an unbeliever to accept Christ—before interest wanes is important, because the interest level will not remain constant. Satan will attempt to lure the person's attention away from Christ through any number of other interests and activities.

The Conviction Level

Some unbelievers, at the conviction level of spiritual development, are under deep conviction for sin. They are restless and miserable. They are searching but do not know what they are searching for or what to do.

Those who are under conviction need the understanding of a caring believer. They do not need to be condemned, regardless of the lifestyle they are living. You may not approve of their lifestyle. You may know that God does not approve of their lifestyle. But your job is not to convict of sin. That is the Holy Spirit's work. Your assignment is to provide what those under conviction are so desperately longing for: the Gospel of His forgiveness and freedom—a new start through faith in Christ. When they come to Christ, *He* will change their lives.

The Conversion Level

Many people have heard the Gospel. The Holy Spirit has convicted them of their sins. They are ready to come to Christ. Now all they need is for someone to simply ask them to accept Christ and take them through the message of the Gospel. They probably already have a basic understanding of the Gospel, but are not sure how to pray and commit their lives to Him. They need a Christian to guide them through the conversion experience.

For some time, Ann, a secretary in a downtown corporate office, had been noticing that Michelle was apparently struggling. Ann spoke kindly to her. As they talked, Ann briefly shared her experience of coming to know Jesus. Michelle's response was another confirmation of the faithfulness of the Holy Spirit. "I prayed this morning that someone would talk to me about God!"

They met at break time, and Ann shared further and prayed with her. Michelle trusted Christ. Ann helped her become grounded in her new relationship with Jesus and helped her find a church home. As you are sensitive to the leading of the Holy Spirit you will discover that many people are like this young woman: ready to receive Christ just as soon as a caring Christian witness takes the time to show them how.

The Growing Level

In the course of daily life, you will meet people who are already brothers or sisters in Christ. As you do so, it will be a joy to discover another Christian friend. You will have the opportunity to participate in your friend's spiritual growth and development. You see, you can encourage one another as you share about Jesus.

Sharing Jesus is needed with our believing friends too. All of us need each other and the mutual support we receive as fellow Christians. As we share, we can rejoice together in the Lord. "And let us consider one another in order to stir up love and good works, not forsaking the assembling of ourselves together, as is the manner of some, but exhorting one another, and so much the more as you see the Day approaching" (Heb. 10:24–25 NKJV).

The Spiritually Declining Level

Some of the people you meet will be experiencing spiritual decline. They have received Christ, joined a church, and at one time lived obedient lives for Christ. But now they are discouraged and defeated. They are not living for Christ and are often bound by an ungodly lifestyle. Their need is for spiritual renewal through confession of sin and yielding their lives anew to Christ.

As you encounter them, you can be used as an instrument of the Holy Spirit to listen to their hurt, pray with them, and point them again to Jesus. You may use the material in Chapter 1 of *People Sharing Jesus* to help the defeated Christian get a "new start." Many simply need the encouragement of a brother or sister in Christ to help restore them to an intimate fellowship with Jesus and the church.

Marla decided to participate in a special *People Sharing Jesus* outreach at her church. Although she regularly taught a group of women in Bible study, this was the first time she had been able to participate in an outreach.

Marla and several others contacted Kathy who met them at her apartment door and welcomed them graciously. As they got acquainted, they talked about her family, interests, and religious background. When asked, "Have you come to know Jesus in a personal way or would you say you are still in the process?" Kathy responded readily. "If you had asked me that question four years ago, I would have told you that I know Jesus and am living for Him." She continued to pour out her story of disappointment and bitterness. Hers was a story of loss of job, financial distress, family conflict, physical illness, and spiritual decline.

The team listened with empathy, shared their own experiences and read from God's Word. After more than an hour of caring ministry and witness, they prayed together. Kathy confessed her bitterness to God and asked His forgiveness. It was a tender time of spiritual renewal of a child of God. Marla made plans with her to encourage her again.

The people you meet will be at varying levels of spiritual development. Whatever their relationship with God, your caring ministry in sharing Christ will be used by the Holy Spirit. To those who are Christians, your sharing will be an encouragement. For those who don't yet know Jesus, your sharing will be used of God to lead them to Christ, either immediately or as part of a process. As a person-centered witness, you must be sensitive to the individual to share Christ at the point of the person's need. You share Jesus with people starting where they are.

Chapter Seven: Personal Review Questions

1. Why is it important to recognize the level of spiritual development of a person as you share the Gospel?

2. How would you describe the primary need of a person at each of the eight spiritual development levels?

   Ignorance:

   Indifference:

   Hostility:

   Interest:

   Conviction:

   Conversion:

   Growing:

   Spiritually Declining.

3. At which level of spiritual development do you think it is more difficult to talk to a person?

Chapter 8

You Never Fail
When You Share Jesus!

You never fail when you share Jesus in the power of the Holy Spirit and leave the results to God. Sharing Jesus *never* fails. This is so important that I want to say it again—a sharing encounter *never* fails. If you share Christ under the leadership of the Holy Spirit and in obedience to Him, He *will* use it for His glory.

Responses to your sharing will vary according to two things: (1) The level of spiritual understanding of the individual, and (2) the leadership of the Holy Spirit.

Some will accept Christ immediately. In the case of others, your first encounter may be preparation for future witness by you and/or someone else.

While your overall purpose is to share Jesus intentionally, you may not know the specific purpose God has in mind until you are involved with the person. Witnessing encounters provide opportunities to discover lost persons and lead them to Christ as well as to nurture those who are already Christians.

Finding the Lost,
Finding Out about Them

Consistently sharing Jesus will enable you to discover peo-

123

123

ple, facts, situations, and needs. What you discover may be the first step in the sharing relationship. As you connect with people and seek to share Jesus, you will learn other important details that will help you understand how to witness.

Determining if a person does not know Christ is the first step in bringing a person to Christ. In conversation, use the guide **FIRM** (**F**amily or friends, **I**nterests, **R**eligion, **M**essage) to help you determine if the person professes to be a Christian. You may be led by the Holy Spirit at that time to share the message of the Gospel. If not, you will continue the conversation to gather details that will aid you in helping the person and in sharing Jesus with them later.

Seek to learn about the person's job, family members, background, and interests. As you get better acquainted, you will likely also find out about any needs that have not been met—family needs, physical needs, emotional needs, and spiritual needs. You will want to follow up later in the light of these needs. Be absolutely sure to pray regularly for the person. Enlist others to join you in prayer and sharing. A team approach is extremely effective in leading people to Christ. Be sure to provide information about the person to any small group or ministry team the person might fit into. The members of these groups can then minister and share along with you. You may be surprised to find that some other Christian with the same occupation or similar experiences may be able to establish instant rapport with the unbeliever.

Reaching people sometimes involves making a home visit or dropping by an office or a place of business to share with the lost person. Make an appointment if possible. If not, drop by anyway, realizing that a visit may not be convenient. If the person is not at home or is too busy at work, your visit can still be a successful one. Leave a note and maybe some Gospel literature (be sure to look at Chapter 11 for some suggestions). Remember that if the Holy

Spirit has placed this person on your heart, then the Holy Spirit is also actively working in that person's heart. If the person is not ready for a direct contact, the Holy Spirit may use your note to stimulate interest. People have been moved to ask Christ into their lives simply through notes left by caring witnesses.

Getting Acquainted

Another purpose of a sharing encounter is to acquaint unbelievers with facts they need to know. The person may need to understand more about the Bible, spiritual relationships, or the church. They may have misconceptions that need to be cleared. Sometimes they simply need to meet a member of the church so that they will see a familiar face if they decide to attend.

Barry had become acquainted with Sid, whom he had met through his work. As he used the acronym **FIRM** (**F**amily, **I**nterests, **R**eligion, **M**essage) to guide the discussion, they talked about Sid's thoughts and feelings. Gradually, Sid began to open up. He confessed that he felt he could never go inside a church building. "I'm not as good as those people!"

Barry took this opportunity to tell Sid about the true nature of a church as the body of Christ. He explained that the people in church were people just like himself, people who had trusted Christ for the forgiveness of their sins. He assured Sid that he would be loved and accepted at church.

Though Sid did not immediately accept Christ, this encounter gave Barry some insights about his new friend. It also provided an opportunity to help Sid understand more about the Gospel and about the real meaning of church.

Having attended church on a Sunday when the preacher spoke on the subject of tithing, Lane had the idea that the church was only interested in his money. In fact, he was so disgusted that he had decided not to go back.

When Phil attempted to share Jesus with him, he discovered the barrier that was standing in the way of his friend's willingness to receive the Gospel. Phil took the time to explain how the money given is used by a church and was able to correct the misconception. Lane showed a growing interest as Phil told him about the satisfaction he felt when _he_ gave and how the church budget operated.

Several sharing encounters may be necessary to remove barriers and to prepare the way for effectively sharing the Gospel. This is all a part of the process of leading someone to Christ.

Sharing honestly and openly about yourself is often invaluable in a witnessing relationship. Lost people are sometimes prejudiced about Christians or don't really know what a Christian is like. As you tell your story and share what Christ means to you, they may be amazed to find that there are more similarities than differences.

Sooner or later, you will have the opportunity to talk about the Gospel. Even if they are not ready to receive Christ, you can sow a seed of truth for the Holy Spirit to nurture. You could share a Bible passage such as John 3:1–18 or follow the Roman Road, which will be explained in a later chapter. Tell them about the church, its mission, objectives, and ministry. Let them know about the programs that may interest them. Leave Gospel literature with them—a booklet, tract, or New Testament—and material about the church.

This encounter—becoming acquainted and laying a foundation—is a valuable part of the process of reaching people for Christ and the church.

Breaking Down Barriers

Many people have allowed barriers to be erected in their hearts and minds against the Gospel and the church, possibly because of some negative experience in the past. They need someone who will care enough to help them put these experiences in proper perspective. The Holy Spirit may use you to help them refocus their thoughts from their disappointment and disillusionment to their need of the Lord. The Lord may use you to help them realize that their relationship with Jesus is the real issue they face.

There are all kinds of barriers that stand in the way of a person's coming to Christ:

The barrier of religion. Some people equate accepting Christ with joining a church. They feel uncomfortable about church; therefore, they think they cannot come to Christ. On the other hand, when people receive Christ, it is natural for them to become a part of the fellowship of the church. But negative attitudes toward the church often become barriers against the Gospel itself.

Financial and social barriers. Some people feel that their clothes are not good enough, that people at church will look down on them, or that they won't fit in. Some may feel that they will be rejected because of the color of their skin.

In actuality, some of these barriers may be very real as far as the church is concerned. Prejudices often not only negate our witness but help to distance us from those who need Jesus. Racial, social, cultural, financial, and other such prejudices have no place in the heart of a Christian or in the life of a church. There is no justification for Christians to practice discrimination in the church, in their relationships—anywhere! The love of Jesus blinds us to differences

127

in people. Through His eyes, we see them as precious and potential brothers and sisters in Christ.

The phrase "no difference" occurs twice in the book of Romans. It is used first with reference to our human sinfulness. "There is no difference, for all have sinned and fall short of the glory of God" (Rom. 3:22–23 NIV). Second, it is used with reference to God's grace extended to all who will call on Him. "For there is no difference between Jew and Gentile—the same Lord is Lord of all and richly blesses all who call on him, for, 'Everyone who calls on the name of the Lord will be saved'" (10:12–13 NIV).

Unbelievers need witnessing Christians who will bridge the gap and reach out to break down the barriers that separate them from Christ.

Arousing Conviction— The Holy Spirit's Job

God also uses sharing encounters to give the Holy Spirit an opportunity to convict a person of their sinfulness and their need of Christ. Before a person can come to Christ, there must be conviction of their sinfulness and a realization of their need of forgiveness through faith in Christ. Some people drift through life with no contact with the Word of God or witnessing Christians. They need someone to share with them the Word of God, which is the sword of the Spirit. The Word is the instrument He uses to convict of sin, righteousness, and judgment. A witness cannot convict an unbeliever; to attempt to do so will only make you seem to be condemning and judgmental. Instead of helping, all you will do is erect further barriers to the Gospel.

A witness cannot convict an unbeliever. Convicting is the work of the Holy Spirit, but he will use the testimony of the believer as a catalyst.

Guiding a Person Through the Conversion Experience

One purpose of a sharing encounter or visit is to guide a seeker through the conversion experience. Some people, whose hearts have been prepared by the Holy Spirit, are ready to make their decisions for Christ at the first encounter. You or someone else may have already shared the Gospel with them earlier. Now they need someone with the spiritual sensitivity to guide them. You can have the joy of taking them spiritually by the hand and leading them in praying and receiving Christ. (I'll show you in Chapter 10.)

After you have led them through the message of the Gospel, suggest that it is time to pray to receive Christ. If it appears that they do not know how to verbalize a prayer, tell them what to say. Lead them to express their repentance for sin and to ask for forgiveness. Then ask them to express commitment to Christ, thanking Him for the assurance that He has come into their heart. Instruct them in how to follow Christ in professing their faith and identifying with a local body of believers.

What a tremendous experience it will be for them and for you as they come to know our wonderful Lord!

Nurturing Christians

Some of the sharing encounters you have will turn out to be for the purpose of nurturing those who are already Christians. As an agent for Christ, your objective is not only to share Christ with the unsaved but to minister to fellow believers.

The Christians you encounter will be at various stages of spiritual development. Some will be growing in faith. You may be able to encourage each other in your service to Christ. You will be mutually blessed and strengthened. Some will be facing problems or challenges. You can pray

129

for them, helping to bear their burdens. You may even be used by God to help resolve a problem.

Other Christians may be new in the area and need prayer and guidance in seeking a church home. Some may have dropped out of church altogether. God will use you to nurture them spiritually and help them become active in the life of a church.

Still other Christians have become defeated and discouraged and have turned away from following Christ. You may be used of God to restore a brother or sister to a life of spiritual victory. Galatians 6:1–2 encourages us: "Brothers, if someone is caught in a sin, you who are spiritual should restore him gently. But watch yourself, or you also may be tempted. Carry each other's burdens, and in this way you will fulfill the law of Christ" (NIV). Ministering to and restoring a Christian who is out of fellowship with Christ and the church is often almost as meaningful to the work of the kingdom of God as leading a lost person to Christ.

Never forget, there is no such thing as an unsuccessful sharing encounter when you go in the name of Christ and for His glory. God is at work in every life to draw each one of them to Jesus and to teach them how to live a victorious Christian life. Once you understand the varying purposes of a sharing encounter, you will go with renewed confidence that you are simply getting in on what God is doing. It's as simple as reaching out to people as He leads us and leaving the results to God.

Chapter Eight: Personal Review Questions

1. What are some of the barriers which keep people you know from being open to the Gospel?

2. How should these barriers be broken down?

Section Three

You *Can* Be
Equipped to
Share Jesus

"I am not ashamed of the gospel, because it is the power of God for the salvation of everyone who believes" (Rom. 1:16 NIV). "So then faith comes by hearing, and hearing by the word of God" (10:17 NKJV).

Using the Bible in personal evangelism is powerful and effective. The purpose of *People Sharing Jesus* is to teach you how to use the Scriptures to share Jesus in a person-centered way. The particular Scriptures to be shared will depend on the needs of the unbeliever as the Holy Spirit leads.

In this section, you'll learn how to share Jesus biblically. And as you share Jesus relationally and biblically, you *will* share Jesus *effectively*. You will learn about the different stages in the process of leading a person to Christ. Chapter 9 will focus on these four stages. I'll give you a logical guide to use in presenting the message in chapter 10. Chapter 11 and the Appendix explore several biblical passages you can use in leading people to Christ.

Understand the Stages of Sharing Jesus

Most people are not led to Jesus in a single encounter with the Gospel. Reaching the lost usually involves both a *process* and a *partnership* in Christian witness. The process almost always includes several Christians who share Jesus before the person ever accepts Him as Savior and Lord.

Each of us is commissioned with the awesome privilege and responsibility of sharing Jesus (Acts 1:8). Each of us who faithfully sows the seed will eventually have the opportunity to lead someone to Christ. But some are more adept at harvesting—leading persons through the new-birth experience—than others. As those who sow and those who reap realize that they are partners in bringing people to Christ, multitudes can be reached. Both sowing and reaping are *essential* to the process.

This process closely corresponds to natural laws used in growing a crop. For example, a wheat farmer must first prepare the soil of a field by breaking it up with a plow so it can receive seed. He then scatters seed until the field is planted. The farmer must then wait for rain and sunshine to provide proper conditions for the seed to germinate and grow into a plant. In time, the plant produces new grain to be harvested. These natural laws were established by God in creation and are woven into the very fabric of the universe. To ignore or avoid them is to risk crop failure. To recognize and abide by them results in a fruitful harvest.

The spiritual principles of sharing Jesus are equally true. To recognize them is to realize that when people receive Christ, it is the work of God. When you lead someone to Christ, you discern what God is doing and cooperate with Him as His instrument in reaching people. Jesus said, "My Father has never stopped working, and that is why I keep on working" (John 5:17). As witnesses for Christ, it is imperative that we work in union with the Father. As we do so, an abundant harvest of hurting people can be reached for Christ.

There are four stages to be recognized in the laws or principles of sowing and reaping that apply to sharing Jesus. These principles work not only for individuals, but also for churches who seek to systematically share Jesus with their communities. I'm going to focus on the individual here. [†] The four stages are done simultaneously and continuously by a church and individual Christian witnesses. They are:

- The Soil-Preparation Stage

- The Sowing Stage

- The Cultivation Stage

- The Harvest Stage

The Soil-Preparation Stage

The "soil" of a person must be prepared to receive the seed of the Gospel. God prepares people to receive His Word through spiritual awakening. Spiritual awakening must begin with the people of God.

134

"God has already begun judging his own people. And if his judgment begins with us, imagine how terrible it will be for those who refuse to obey his message. The Scriptures say, 'If good people barely escape, what will happen to sinners and to others who don't respect God?'" (1 Peter 4:17–18). As God's people, we are being called upon to repent and turn to Him as never before.

When God's revived people respond to Him in surrender and obedience, they permeate their community with the presence of the living Lord. As they go about their daily lives, they become like salt to the earth and light to the world. A Christ-filled, Christ-centered life influences unbelievers for God, affirming His presence and power.

After the coming of the Holy Spirit at Pentecost, the lives of the followers of Christ were changed to reflect the presence of the risen Lord. Acts 2:12 captures their excitement: "Everyone was excited and confused. Some of them even kept asking each other, 'What does all this mean?'"

In the climate of spiritual awakening in the church after Pentecost, the lives of believers impacted the world around them. They continued "praising God and enjoying the favor of all the people. And the Lord added to their number daily those who were being saved" (Acts 2:47 NIV). Spiritual awakening in the church overflowed to permeate the community and create a climate of receptivity to the Gospel.

When Peter and John were brought before the Sanhedrin, Peter concluded his witness for Christ by saying, "Only Jesus has the power to save! His name is the only one in all the world that can save anyone" (4:12). His words, backed by his godly lifestyle, drew the following response: "When they saw the courage of Peter and John and realized that they were unschooled, ordinary men, they were astonished and they took note that these men had been with Jesus" (v. 13 NIV). The change that God has wrought in your life affirms the Gospel and prepares the soil of a community to receive the seed of the Gospel.

135

Since spiritual awakening in the lives of believers is critical to preparing the soil for seed sowing, how can this awakening be experienced? The answer is simple: We must deal with our sins, repent, and yield to Christ. The sin of focusing our attention on ourselves and our own needs and desires leads us into self-centeredness rather than Christ-centeredness and produces a loss of vision for reaching others for Him.

God promises: "If my people, who are called by my name, will humble themselves and pray and seek my face and turn from their wicked ways, then will I hear from heaven and will forgive their sin and will heal their land. Now my eyes will be open and my ears attentive to the prayers offered in this place" (2 Chron. 7:14–15 NIV).

I was part of a church on the Gulf Coast when God sent a spirit of renewal in the midst of terrible personal tragedy. A fourteen-year-old boy named Eddie had been drowned in the nearby bayou during a torrential rain the week before.

Though we missed the main force of the hurricane that spawned the downpour, the waters of every bay and inlet were up and raging. Eddie and his brothers had constructed a raft of Styrofoam and were floating in the rushing waters of the bayou. As they approached the spillway, the raft broke up. Two of the boys made it out of water in spite of the steep concrete banks. But Eddie could not get out. He clung to a piece of Styrofoam from the raft, calling for help.

The other boys ran home to tell their dad, Leroy. Leroy jumped into his pickup truck and raced to the bayou. With Eddie floating just out of reach, Leroy ran back to the truck and got a rope. "I threw him the rope, but the rope was too short," Eddie's dad lamented. "And I saw my boy go over the spillway into the deep waters below. We found his body about three o'clock the next morning."

When Leroy told me the heartrending story, I was seated across a desk from him at the funeral home. A chill went down my spine and tears came to my eyes as I visualized the boy screaming, "Help me, somebody help me! I can't hold on much longer!" I could see not only Eddie, but the unbelieving multitudes of our city and the world clinging in desperation to some fragile thread of hope. I could see us as Christians throwing out ropes—ropes too short to reach our world in this day.

Two weeks earlier, Eddie had accepted Christ through the witness of some people at our church. Leroy asked me to participate in Eddie's funeral. And in the days surrounding the funeral, the entire family and several friends and neighbors received Christ. They were all at church for the first time on Sunday.

As I shared Eddie's story with the congregation that day, I told them about the rope that was too short. Then God led me to apply the story by saying, "We Christians live with a lost community around us. They are holding onto whatever they can to survive. They're reaching out for anything that offers hope. They're crying, 'Help me. Won't someone help me? I can't hold on much longer!' And we Christians are all too often throwing out ropes that are too short to reach the people of our world in our day!"

At 11:50 A.M., I began to close the service with an appeal for people to come to Christ. Though the service usually concluded around noon, this Sunday the service was still going at 1:30 P.M. as people streamed down the aisle to confess their sins and receive Christ as their Savior. Several times I encouraged the people to feel free to leave or to sit down if they needed to, but we would keep the invitation open as long as God was moving. And still they came.

Some forty people confessed Christ that day. Many others made significant decisions and experienced personal renewal. The spirit of renewal continued for years. Hundreds of Christians were equipped to share Jesus. As they shared Him in the marketplace and in their daily lives, as well as through the organized outreach efforts of the church, thousands more were brought to Christ. Within a year, Leroy alone had led at least fifty people to Christ. Leroy, his family, and the church had found that there is a Rope that is not too short. It is Jesus who left heaven to come to this sin-infested earth to reach every person with His love and forgiveness.

As I studied the circumstances of the revival, I discovered that the church had been in decline for some time. The people had been discouraged and disgruntled. Discord and disunity had prevailed. But a small group of members had covenanted to pray and seek God for revival. They had met for several years every Tuesday morning at 5:00 A.M. to pray. God moved in answer to their prayers. The lives of multitudes were changed. The entire city was impacted as God moved in the lives of His people. Within the next few years, the church quadrupled in size.

As God's people pray, we open our lives for all He desires to do in and through us.

God told His people in Jeremiah's day, and He is telling us today: "Break up your unplowed ground and do not sow among thorns" (4:3 NIV).

As a farmer breaks up the hard surface soil of his field to rid it of weeds and prepare for sowing the seed, the people of God must break up the hard soil of their disobedient, rebellious spirit toward God. Through prayer and repentance, we must seek the Lord and realize His mission. Christ is the head of the Church (Col. 1:18)! The Church as a body and its individual members must line up under His headship. Whatever stands in the way of Christ's being exalted as Head and the Church moving under His lordship must be confessed and forsaken.

God responds to seeking hearts. "You will seek me and find me when you seek me with all your heart" (Jer. 29:13 NIV).

In the days of Samuel, too, God's people were in a spiritually deplorable state. "In those days Israel had no king; everyone did as he saw fit" (Judg. 21:25 NIV). When we do what is right in our own sight, it will not lead us to God. As Samuel ministered and God worked, "all the people of Israel mourned and sought after the LORD" (1 Sam. 7:2 NIV).

Samuel called the people to repentance. "And [he] said to the whole house of Israel, 'If you are returning to the LORD with all your hearts, then rid yourselves of the foreign gods and the Ashtoreths and commit yourselves to the LORD and serve him only, and he will deliver you out of the hand of the Philistines'" (v. 3). Israel did repent, praying and confessing their sins. And God moved mightily in spiritual awakening. He delivered his people and routed the Philistines from the land. Samuel set up a stone of witness and called it "Ebenezer," declaring "The Lord helped us."

When we repent, seek the Lord, and obey Him, God will act mightily in our behalf. He wants to give revival. He is ready to do so. In fact, He has been ready for a long time. He is waiting for us to get ready and turn to Him. He wants to help us as He helped the people in Samuel's day. He wants to use us to call the multitudes to Himself.

Spiritual awakening will enable Christians to act as God's agents as He breaks up the unplowed ground of a community to prepare the soil for the seed of His Word.

The Sowing Stage

Unlike the order in the process of farming, the seed-sowing of the Word of God is done simultaneously with the preparation of the soil. Take note of four truths regarding seed-sowing:

Sowing with an Eye to the Harvest

I enjoy gardening. I enjoy getting outside and tilling the soil. I especially like garden-fresh tomatoes, so I prepare the soil and plant tomato seed. As I plant the seed, I am thinking of the delicious red tomatoes that will be on our table in a few months. Now, if I did not believe there would be a harvest, I would never plant the seed. Visualizing the harvest motivates me to sow the seed. I know that if I plant the seed, cultivate, water, fertilize, and nurture the tomato plant, I will eventually be eating delicious tomatoes from my garden. But if I do not go through the process of doing the gardening essentials, I will gather no fruit.

The same is true in sharing Jesus with people. If you sow, you will reap. The reverse is also true: no sowing—no reaping. Galatians 6:9 promises, "Let us not become weary in doing good, for at the proper time we will reap a harvest if we do not give up" (NIV).

If we continue to faithfully sow the seed of God's Word, the joyous day of bringing in the fruit will come. "He who goes out weeping, carrying seed to sow, / will return with songs of joy, carrying sheaves with him" (Ps. 126:6 NIV). The sheaves are the harvest! They are the bundles of wheat with their heads of grain to be threshed and eaten or sold. They are the end result of all the hard work of preparing the soil, planting the seed, cultivating the crop, and laboring to bring in the fruit. Focusing on the harvest will help you to keep on sharing Jesus.

Saturation—The Seed-Sowing Principle

Interestingly, unlike the farmer who sows seed, the witnessing believer will reap as the seed of the Gospel is being sown. The moment the seed is sown, some will be ready to receive Christ. Usually, when this happens, someone else has previously sown the Gospel seed. Then the truth Jesus gave will be realized: "Even now the harvest workers are receiving their reward by gathering a harvest that brings eternal life. Then everyone who planted the seed and everyone who harvests the crop will celebrate together. So the saying proves true, 'Some plant the seed, and others harvest the crop.' I am sending you to harvest crops in fields where others have done all the hard work" (John 4:36–38).

Sowing God's Word

That which must be sown in the hearts and minds of the lost is God's Word. In Psalm 126:6 (NIV), the Word is "seed to sow." Other seed harvested by a Hebrew farmer might be sold or made into flour and eaten by the family. But the the "seed to sow" was carefully guarded and reserved to be planted. Even in times of hunger, the planting seed would not be eaten. If they had no seed to sow, there would be no harvest in the future. Our seed is the Word of God. It is, as the King James Version so magnificently translates it, "precious seed."

The farmer sows cotton to harvest cotton, corn to harvest corn, and wheat to harvest wheat. The Word of God produces a spiritual harvest. We reap in kind as we have sown. "Do not be deceived: God cannot be mocked. A man reaps what he sows. The one who sows to please his sinful nature, from that nature will reap destruction; the one who sows to please the Spirit, from the Spirit will reap eternal life" (Gal. 6:7 NIV). "So then faith comes by hearing, and hearing by the word of God" (Rom. 10:17 NKJV). Sow the seed of the Word of God. It will bring forth a harvest!

Reaping in Proportion to Seed Sown

The proportion of the harvest will be directly related to the amount of seed-sowing done. "Remember this: Whoever sows sparingly will also reap sparingly, and whoever sows generously will also reap generously.... Now, he who supplies seed to the sower and bread for food will also supply and increase your store of seed and will enlarge the harvest of your righteousness" (2 Cor. 9:6, 10 NIV).

My dad was a farmer in West Texas where cotton was king and cattle was the rival industry. It is a flat, sometimes barren, sometimes fertile land. Rain is the questionable factor as far as productivity of harvest is concerned. The entire year revolves around harvest time in fall. In the winter my dad plowed and prepared the field carefully for planting. In the spring he planted the cottonseed. God watered the seed with rain and warmed it with the sun. Summer was a time of diligent cultivation. Harvest came in the fall. It was a time of hard work, but a time of great satisfaction when the crops were gathered.

Suppose that one spring my dad had decided that the rigorous procedure of soil preparation, planting, and cultivation was senseless. What he enjoyed was the harvest. So he decided to focus his attention and efforts on the harvest!

During the cold winter, instead of the grueling labor of breaking up the soil, suppose he had taken an extended vacation to the warm beaches of Florida. He enjoyed it so much that he stayed through planting time. Then, because of the unpleasant heat of summer, suppose he had spent the cultivating time in the cool mountains of Colorado, planning to be home just in time to enjoy the fruit of harvest.

What do you think he would have found when he arrived home in the fall? A bountiful harvest of cotton? No! If he had ignored the law of the harvest, there would have been only a few scattered cotton plants that had come up voluntarily.

No soil preparation, no planting, no cultivating equal no harvest!

Keeping on Sowing

Persistence in sharing the Gospel is essential for a continuous harvest. "And let us not grow weary while doing good, for in due season we shall reap if we do not lose heart" (Gal. 6:9 NKJV).

The continual and consistent sowing of seed (sharing Jesus) is not easy. Satan will use all kinds of events and activities to consume the time and energy of Christians. He will even use many good things to crowd out the one thing most necessary to reach unbelievers—personal witnessing. Witnessing requires the discipline of commitment to intentional evangelization of the church's entire surrounding area.

Paul instructed young Timothy: "I can't impress this on you too strongly. God is looking over your shoulder, Christ himself is the Judge, with the final say on everyone, living and dead. He is about to break into the open with His rule, so proclaim the message with intensity; keep on your watch. Challenge, warn, and urge your people. Don't ever quit. Just keep it simple" (2 Tim. 4:2 ††). Sharing Christ must be done when it is convenient and when it is not convenient, so "keep on your watch" for opportunities. In other words, you must call upon all of the resources available to you through the Holy Spirit to keep on sowing until *every person* finds forgiveness and freedom through faith in Christ.

After he met Jesus, Paul was committed to sharing Jesus with others. He engaged in the trade of tent making as he went from place to place, sharing Jesus on the way and in the marketplace. He began in Ephesus sharing Christ in the Jewish synagogue, where he continued for three months. When he was driven out of the synagogue, he moved to the lecture hall of Tyrannus in the marketplace of Ephesus. There he held daily discussions about Jesus and equipped believers to share Jesus (Acts 19).

Later, Paul reviewed his lifestyle of evangelism and

church-starting with the Ephesian elders: "You know that I have not hesitated to preach anything that would be helpful to you but have taught you publicly and from house to house. I have declared to both Jews and Greeks that they must turn to God in repentance and have faith in our Lord Jesus. . . . Remember that for three years I never stopped warning each of you night and day with tears" (Acts 20:20, 31 NIV).

The result of the ministry of evangelizing and equipping believers to evangelize was "that all the Jews and Greeks who lived in the province of Asia heard the word of the Lord" (19:10 NIV). The church of Ephesus grew mightily in number and in spirit. Through the lives of the believers as they were scattered, the Gospel permeated all the surrounding area. What an impact was made in the first century through the persistent sharing of believers.

The strategy of evangelism has not changed. Like Paul, every believer is on a mission for Christ to share His Word, empowered by the mighty power of the Holy Spirit. Multitudes can be reached today. Yet the tendency we have is to drift away from a daily lifestyle of sharing Jesus, as did the believers in Ephesus. By the end of the first century, Jesus gave John a message to the church of Ephesus: "Yet I hold this against you: You have forsaken your first love. Remember the height from which you have fallen! Repent and do the things you did at first" (Rev. 2:4–5 NIV).

Ephesus had left its first work. The people had gradually moved away from their first priority of reaching people with the Gospel. Their first love had grown cold. Jesus called them to repent and resume doing the things they had done when their faith was new. They were to honor their first priority of taking the Gospel to every person. Evidence reveals that they did *not* repent and return to the priority of lifestyle evangelism. Today, the city of Ephesus lies in ruins. The church of Ephesus is nonexistent. It is difficult to find a believer in that entire area.

Continuing to share Jesus and saturate our communities with the Gospel must be done at all costs. It costs time, money, and involvement to reach hurting, lost people. The priority of evangelistic witness should be tangibly translated into allotting time to pray for those who don't know Jesus, to relate to them, and to share the Gospel and lead them to salvation. Reaching people will require the discipline of being alert to unscheduled "divine appointments" and spending time with unbelievers in order to share Jesus with them.

The Cultivation Stage

Believers obediently share Christ and sow Gospel seed. But cultivation is the work of the Holy Spirit. When we attempt to do the work of the Spirit, we are spectacularly ineffective. As believers witness, the Spirit works to cultivate the hearts of those who don't know Him.

The Holy Spirit works through all types of circumstances in the lives of unbelievers. In fact, circumstances provide opportunities for the work of cultivation. God often permits both blessing and difficulty to come into the lives of people in order to reveal His love. Through circumstances, the Holy Spirit cultivates a realization of the need for God in the lives of lost people.

The Holy Spirit works though disappointment. In John 4:1–42, Jesus dealt with the needs of the woman at the well. After four unsuccessful marriages, she was no doubt suffering greatly from a sense of failure and loss of self-esteem. She had evidently given up on marriage and had begun living with a man who was not her husband. She needed forgiveness and a new start. As the Holy Spirit drew her to the living water, Jesus changed her life.

All of us face disappointments and hurts in life. People

145

who have not experienced the forgiveness and presence of Christ begin to recognize their need for His help. Through their need, the Holy Spirit cultivates within their hearts an openness to the Gospel. Believers have an opportunity to meet them at the point of their need with the Word of God.

When Michael lost his job, he and his wife, Lauren, became increasingly distressed as their savings dwindled. During this time, their family became known by some members of a local church through a community outreach the church conducted on a Sunday afternoon. Church members loved this family with the love of Jesus Christ and responded to the need by providing food, clothing for the children, and other essentials. As Christians from the church ministered, they found a receptive atmosphere for sowing the seed of the Gospel.

Ultimately, the whole family trusted Christ and came into the church. One of the members assisted Michael in finding another job, where he soon regained financial stability. In reflecting on their experience, Michael said, "We did not enjoy the difficulty, but we're glad it happened. Through it all, we came to realize our need of Christ. We received Him and found wonderful Christian friends, too. Had we not become destitute, we might have gone on as we were. What has happened to us has been worth everything we had to endure."

The Holy Spirit works through sickness. In Mark 5:25–34, a sick woman who had spent all her money in trying to find a cure for a persistent bleeding problem was drawn to the Great Physician by the Holy Spirit. She reached out to Him in her need, and Jesus healed her and gave her peace.

A time of illness is an opportunity for loving ministry by believers. It often opens the door for witness. Sobered by the realization that they can do nothing to help themselves, people afflicted by illness are often actively reassessing their values. Shawn, an aviation expert whose life was centered on his job and the pursuit of pleasure, became open to Jesus when he was diagnosed as having leukemia. Ginny turned to the church for prayer and became open to the Gospel when she developed cancer.

The Holy Spirit works through the death of a friend or family member.

When Jairus's daughter died, the Holy Spirit drew him to the One who is the Resurrection and the Life. Jesus brought the power of life into the home, raising the child from the dead (Mark 5:21–43).

Many are drawn to Christ by the Holy Spirit when a loved one dies. A caring witness can lead the grieving person to the God of all comfort. "Praise God, the Father of our Lord Jesus Christ! The Father is a merciful God, who always gives us comfort. He comforts us when we are in trouble, so that we can share that same comfort with others in trouble" (2 Cor. 1:3–4). Before the drowning incident I shared earlier, Eddie's father and mother, Leroy and Bobbie, had been bitter toward Christ and the church. Initial visits by church visitors had been rebuffed, though Eddie's parents did allow their children to go to church. When their son Eddie drowned, however, Leroy and Bobbie became open to the ministry of the church and trusted Christ.

The Holy Spirit works through the birth of a child.
When Enoch's first child was born, the new father began to walk with God (Gen. 5:21–22). As I was sharing Jesus with a young father after the birth of his first child, he said, "Things are going to have to be different now. We need to be in church." The young man and his wife received Christ and joined the church. The Holy Spirit used the arrival of the new baby to soften the daddy's heart and convict him of his responsibility.

In recognition of the opportunity to meet needs and share Jesus after the birth of a baby, my wife and several other women began a "Baby Brigade." They secured the names and addresses of new parents from the birth announcement section of the local newspaper and took a small gift to each new mother in the community after she came home from the hospital. The new mothers welcomed the visit and the personal attention. The result was that many young-adult families were reached for Christ and the church.

The Holy Spirit works through guilt in a life. In the incidents described in Acts 7:54–60 and 9:4–5, Saul of Tarsus became open to Jesus through the heaviness of his own guilt. He watched the coats of those who hurled the stones that killed Stephen. He heard Stephen cry out while they were stoning him, "I see heaven open and the Son of Man standing at the right side of God" (Acts 7:56). Then, as he was dying, he shouted, "Lord, don't blame them for what they have done" (Acts 7:60). Saul reacted with fury! He gained permission and sought out Christians to persecute, arrest, and jail. As he started toward Damascus to seek out and arrest Christians—no doubt he was conscience-stricken over his part in the stoning of Stephen—Saul was vulnerable to the Holy Spirit's convicting power. Dazed by the blinding light on the road to Damascus and hearing a voice speaking to him, Saul acknowledged Christ as "Lord" and surrendered his life to him.

The Holy Spirit cultivates hearts through keeping their sins ever before them. Many bear heavy burdens of unresolved conflict and unforgiven sin. Caring ministry and sharing open the door to reach the guilt-ridden for Christ. Personally sharing Jesus with individuals works in concert with the Holy Spirit in leading them to experience God's forgiveness. The burden of guilt is removed as they repent and receive Christ.

The Holy Spirit works continually to draw people to Christ (John 6:44). He enlightens the minds of unbelievers to understand the things of God (16:13), for they are in spiritual darkness and cannot understand the Gospel until the Holy Spirit illuminates their sin-darkened minds. The Holy Spirit works by convicting the heart of the unbeliever (vv. 8–11). He convicts of the sin of unbelief, the righteousness of Jesus, and impending judgment.

The Holy Spirit reveals Jesus to the hearts of humans (v. 14). Before a person can experience salvation, Jesus must become real. It is then that the sharing of the plan of salvation can be used by the Spirit to work the miracle of regeneration. It is the Spirit who births a person into the kingdom of God (3:3–5).

The Holy Spirit works through the ministry of caring Christians. In Matthew 25:35–36, Jesus admonished His followers to minister to those in need. Practical, caring ministry opens hearts to the Word of God.

The Holy Spirit works through the blessings and successes of life. At the beginning of a new year, a successful medical doctor committed his life to Christ. The doctor made the statement to the Christian who witnessed to him, "God has blessed my life in such a way that I realize I can do nothing without Him!" He was right. "God's kindness leads [you] to repentance" (Rom. 2:4b NIV).

Just as the doctor expressed, daily God blesses us with life, family, friends, and jobs. Our health, homes, and hope are all results of His graciousness. Even when reversals come and we lose our jobs, health, or even our loved ones, God reaches out to us to provide His presence, strength, and daily provision. Apart from His sustaining grace we could not arise from bed and begin the day each morning.

You are an instrument for the Holy Spirit to use. It is important to remember that the Holy Spirit uses the witness of believers as He cultivates hearts. The witness must be faithful to continue to share Jesus. Being sensitive to what the Holy Spirit is doing in the person's life, consider using the following suggestions:

- Develop a personal prayer list of lost friends and acquaintances.

- Stay in touch with the person.

- Make a phone call or stop by from time to time.

- Write notes on special occasions or just to express your concern.

- Invite the person to be your guest for lunch.

- Invite him or her to go with you to Bible study and worship.

- Cooperate with the Holy Spirit as He cultivates.

- Don't over visit.

If the person shows a lack of interest, make less frequent contact. Pray more intensely and allow some time to elapse. As barriers are broken down and interest develops, increase contact. Pray daily for the unbelievers on your prayer list. Remember that the Holy Spirit is always there cultivating their hearts and lives. Creatively explore other ways to be used by the Holy Spirit to reach people for Christ.

The Harvest Stage

Harvest time is the time of gathering in people to Jesus. Relatively few of the unsaved will come to the churches to be reached, however. The harvest of lost people is out there in the world. To reach them, we must go where they are. Jesus did. "And Jesus went about all the cities and villages, teaching in their synagogues, preaching the Gospel of the kingdom, and healing every sickness and every disease among the people" (Matt. 9:35 NKJV).

Jesus did not overlook anyone and neither should we. He went to the large cities, the small villages, and the open countryside—wherever people were. He combated the three deadly enemies of humanity—ignorance, sin, and disease. To combat the enemy of ignorance, he taught the truth of God. To know the truth is to be liberated. To combat the enemy of sin, he preached the kingdom of God. The rule of God in a heart delivers from sin. To combat the enemy of disease, he healed. The ministry of healing relieves suffering. You and I can emulate the model of ministry demonstrated by Jesus.

A compassionate heart is the key to reaching the multitudes. "But when He saw the multitudes, He was moved with compassion for them, because they were weary and scattered, like sheep having no shepherd" (v. 36). Jesus' heart was torn by the sight of hurting, destitute people. They were like sheep who had wandered with their heavy burdens until they collapsed. They were scattered abroad, far from the fold. There were no shepherds to care for them.

Where were the shepherds? They were all congregated at Jerusalem, busily involved in their religious activities while the sheep stumbled and fell.

All of us as Christians are shepherds to give spiritual nurture, to support, and to share Jesus with those around us. As has already been shown in Chapter 5, we can live in the midst of people who are hurting and in need and never really see them. A heart of compassion like Jesus' will make us sensitive to the deep spiritual needs of those around us. We will develop an eye for the harvest.

With a heart breaking for the people, Jesus said, "The harvest truly is plentiful, but the laborers are few. Therefore pray the Lord of the harvest to send out laborers into His harvest" (Matt. 9:37–38 NKJV).

The harvest belongs to the Lord. He is the owner of the harvest. What confidence this gives us as laborers who go into the harvest to witness. The laborer is simply to gather in people for the Lord. The Christian goes with the authority of the Lord who owns the harvest.

The harvest is a treasure to the Lord. Every person is a treasure to God with glorious potential. Carl was a drug-using, black-jacketed motorcycle rider. Through his drug habit, he became infected with hepatitis. A caring Christian literally moved into Carl's home and nursed him back to health. During the extended illness, he shared Jesus with Carl and led him to Christ. Carl went back to work a changed man. As he grew in Christ, he became concerned about others and their relationship with Christ. He began to distribute New Testaments where he worked. At first, nobody would take one from him. So he brought a box of New Testaments and left them on the table in the break room. Soon the box was emptied by Carl's coworkers.

Carl asked his boss to permit him to begin a noon Bible study. His boss was shocked. "Carl, you've been in my office for every kind of reason. Now, *this!* What few Christians we have here, I'm not going to turn over to you and let you ruin them!"

However, in a short while, Carl's boss could see the difference Jesus had made in him and did permit him to begin a Bible study at the plant. In the months to come, Carl led scores to Christ. The entire area where he worked was permeated with an influence for Christ. Carl was a rich treasure to the kingdom of God. Many, like Carl, are wandering aimlessly without God. God has a glorious purpose for them. We must reach them for Christ.

The harvest must be harvested quickly. The harvest is plentiful and ready for reaping. But if left as it is, it will soon be wasted. Jesus spoke about the urgency of the harvest. "Do you not say, 'Four months more and then the harvest'? I tell you, open your eyes and look at the fields! They are ripe for harvest" (John 4:35 NIV).

The danger is that the harvest may waste in the fields for the lack of laborers. Opportunity will soon be past. One by one, unbelievers will die. The soon coming of Jesus will end the possibility of the church's reaching them for salvation. The time is now!

"Therefore pray the Lord of the harvest to send out laborers into His harvest" (Matt. 9:38 NKJV) was the instruction of Jesus. Pray, then go yourself. It is impossible to pray with sincerity for unbelievers without becoming involved in reaching them.

A friend of Martin Luther once dreamed about a lone reaper attempting to gather in the harvest. In his dream, as he drew near the reaper, he saw that it was Luther. Luther's friend awakened with a start and said, "I must leave my prayers and get to the work."

The harvest is a time of rejoicing. The Jews of Jesus' day celebrated the gathering of the fruit with a harvest feast. How much more the joy is multiplied when the fruit is the lives of people for whom Christ died.

When people receive Christ, there is joy among the laborers. Jesus said that the sower and the reaper rejoice together. There is nothing that energizes and gladdens the heart of a Christian more than leading a person to Christ. Multitudes of petty church problems would be resolved if members would involve themselves in the mission of Jesus to reach the unreached. The priorities of Jesus would become the priorities of the church.

When people ask Christ to come into their lives and forgive them of their sin, there is joy in the presence of the

Lord. The salvation of an unbeliever causes heaven to rejoice and brings joy to the church. Even the angels rejoice. "God's angels are happy when even one person turns to him" (Luke 15:10). The only activity recorded in the Bible by which you and I can cause rejoicing in heaven is bringing people to know Jesus Christ.

Each of us should make sharing Jesus with others a priority.

Most people will not be reached quickly or easily, however. Time is required to reach many of them. If it's possible, you should seriously consider participating in your church's regular outreach to visit the community. Some people will never be reached without a systematic plan.

I've found these general principles to be helpful in contacting people to reap God's harvest.

1. Contact people at a time when they are most likely to be at home—early evening, late morning, or early afternoon on Saturday and Sunday. Daytime contacts are usually better for senior adults.

2. Make an appointment ahead of time. This is considerate and may save time. You may phone for an appointment a day or two before you plan to come, or call and ask permission to come a few minutes before you leave. If the person will not grant an appointment, visit by phone. People can be led to Christ and reached for the church over the telephone.

3. Drop by a home or place of business. Drop-by visits are sometimes effective. You have to be sensitive to the community in which you live. People may be annoyed when drop-by visits are made too often and without sensitivity. Making visits with sensitivity to the people,

with appropriate timing, and in connection with an event will minimize the possibility of offending them.

Suggestions for a drop-by visit:

1. Be courteous. Introduce yourself. Ask for permission to visit. If the time appears to be inconvenient, ask if you may come at another time.

2. If the person does not invite you in, chat briefly at the door.

3. Take with you something meaningful to give the person you've come to see—a modern version of a *People Sharing Jesus* New Testament, an audiotape of a key message your pastor has preached, brochures from your church, tracts, Gospel booklets, and information about specific events that have been scheduled.

4. If the person is not at home, leave a personal note, biblical material, and information about your church on the door. People can be reached through such notes.

5. When the person you came to see is not in, try sharing with the person next door or in the next office. Introduce yourself and your teammate. Say something like, "We are from _____ Church. We came by to visit the _____ family next door. Do you know when they may be home?" (Wait for an answer.) "May we take a moment to share with you?"

   After an attempt to see the person who was not home, my secretary and her friend were driving away from the house when the secretary said, "We forgot to go next door." Instantly, they turned the car around and went back to knock on that door. Five people accepted Christ and joined the church the very next

Sunday. The divine appointment for the sharing team was next door!

6. Do not forget the person. Pray for him or her. Do not make yours a one-time visit. Make periodic contacts. God is at work to reach the person. Be sensitive to the changes and openness the Holy Spirit will bring about.

Sharing Jesus is every Christian's job. We must equip ourselves and others through organized outreach and daily lifestyle witness to go into the harvest. This process requires time and effort, but the rewards are infinitely worthwhile! Remember, we are part of that powerful team of three that God uses to bring people to Himself: the Word of God, the work of the Holy Spirit, and the sharing of the believer. God wants to use *you* to share Jesus.

† I've written a book on how churches can systematically share Jesus with their communities; it's called *Total Church Life*. Ask for it at your favorite Christian bookstore.

†† Eugene H. Peterson, *The Message: The New Testament in Contemporary English* (Colorado Springs, CO: NavPress, 1993), 449.

Chapter Nine: Personal Review Questions

1. This chapter speaks of the preparing of the soil as the breaking up of the hardened attitudes and acts of disobedience of the individual or church prior to being used by God. When you think of revival, what is the first thing that comes into your mind? From your experience and understanding, what are the conditions necessary for true revival?

2. The phrase *sowing with an eye to the harvest* is used in this book. What do you think this means in personal evangelism?

3. Looking back to Chapter 3, how do you see the team relationship of the Word of God, the Holy Spirit, and the believer fitting in to the analogy of the stages of sharing Jesus?

4. How would you describe the stages of witnessing—*preparing the ground, sowing, watering, harvesting?* As you share your faith, what should happen in each of these stages?

5. Like that of a farmer, the attitude of the person sharing Jesus should be to start with the end in sight, looking forward to the harvest. How would this attitude change the way you would prepare the ground, sow, and water? Which is more important: sowing, watering, or reaping the harvest?

6. What does it mean to share Jesus intentionally?

Understand the Seven Steps in Leading a Person to Christ

Leading people to faith in Christ is such a joy. Remember, you're part of a mighty team of three: the Word of God, the work of the Holy Spirit, and the witness of the believer. Generally there are two points of greatest challenge in sharing the Gospel. The first is when you begin to share the plan of salvation. The second is when you ask the person to pray and receive Christ. You may feel the temptation to stop short of presenting the Gospel or of asking the person to pray. Remember, if you don't give the person a chance to respond, you haven't fulfilled your assignment of sharing Jesus with them. Period.

You may feel the tension as you actually launch into the plan of salvation or reach the moment of decision with the person to whom you are witnessing. The tension comes from several sources. Satan resists anyone coming to Christ. He will attempt to distract you in any way possible. He will use interruptions and interferences in an attempt to divert you from your objective. Fear is another source of tension. The fear of not knowing what to say or do may silence the witness or cause hesitation.

Therefore, it is important to know a step-by-step process by which to guide someone through the conversion experience. Simply to know the steps that can be taken will give confidence and relieve much of the tension. These steps can be put into practice or laid aside. While it is helpful to have a procedure in mind, it is far more important to follow the Holy Spirit as He leads. The Holy Spirit may prepare the person to receive Christ right away. But it is more likely that He will bring conviction and draw the person to Christ gradually as the Gospel is shared over a period of time.

The following is a seven-step process that may be used:

The steps may be thought of as a stairway. With the help of the witness, the lost person is assisted in climbing the stairway as he or she moves from being lost toward receiving Christ.

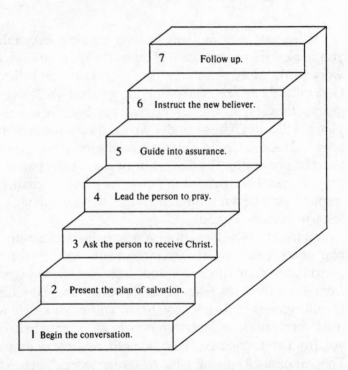

7 Follow up.

6 Instruct the new believer.

5 Guide into assurance.

4 Lead the person to pray.

3 Ask the person to receive Christ.

2 Present the plan of salvation.

1 Begin the conversation.

Step 1: Begin the Conversation

Since the Holy Spirit is always at work drawing the lost to Christ, you know that He has preceded your visit. The goal is to be sensitive to the person's needs as you present the plan of salvation.

- Go in the spirit of prayer, but rely on the Holy Spirit! He will lead in developing an opening for presenting the Gospel.

- Utilize the conversation guide in Chapter 4. Guide the conversation, using the acronym **FIRM** (Friends or Family, Interests, Religion, Message). Discuss family, interests, religious background. Then ask permission to share the message. "Have you come to know Jesus in a personal way, or would you say you are still in the process?" is a nonthreatening way to move into the message. Ask, "May I share with you how you can come to know Him?"

- As you begin to share Jesus, you may need to probe to determine the degree of openness to the Gospel on the part of the person to whom you are witnessing. Your probing may be compared to trying a door. Your probing is like knocking on the door. You probe by asking questions and waiting for responses. You may ask questions like, "Have you thought much lately about your relationship with Jesus Christ?" or "Has anyone shared with you about Jesus and how to come to know Him?" As you approach a door, you will not know whether or not it will open. As you try the door and find it open, move through and continue to share until you face a door that will not open. If the door is locked, don't attempt to break it down. As you probe, the person may express resistance to your sharing. You may ask if he or she will share their opinion about some aspect of what you have been discussing. If the person appears to be annoyed, you may change the subject and wait for another time to attempt to share Jesus. Follow the Holy Spirit's guidance in trying another door or wait until the door opens.

Luis had an evening engagement to attend, but decided to take a few minutes after work to run by the hospital and visit Juan, a friend of a friend. Luis made a brief, cordial visit, and had prayer. As he turned to leave, he thought, *I should ask Juan to trust Jesus.*

Returning to the bedside, he said very tenderly, "Juan, we have talked about Jesus at other times, but I've never asked you to trust Him as your own Savior and Lord. How do you feel about receiving Christ now?"

Juan responded with complete openness, "I'm ready to do it now!" The presence of God filled the hospital room as both of them prayed and Juan received Christ.

Luis "tried the door" in sharing Jesus with Juan and found it open. If the door had not opened, Luis could have asked, "What do you feel is standing in the way of your trusting Christ?" and continued to discuss his response.

Step 2: Present the Plan of Salvation

In presenting the plan of salvation, you will want to prayerfully discern the method to use and the Scriptures to share. The approach you take should be determined by two primary factors: the guidance of the Holy Spirit, and the need and level of understanding of the person to whom you are witnessing. Often, the Holy Spirit gives impressions as to the direction or approach to take as you begin to share. Factors involved will be the amount of time available for sharing, the background and biblical knowledge of the person with whom you are sharing, and the person's apparent level of interest. You can pray for the Holy Spirit's guidance and empowerment and be sensitive to the person as you are sharing, then follow the impressions the Spirit gives.

Use the approach that will be most meaningful. Paul spoke of this in his letter to the Corinthians: "I have become all things to all men so that by all possible means I might save some" (1 Cor. 9:22 NIV). Several approaches that I will show you in more detail in Chapter 11 and in the Appendix are as follows:

- A witnessing booklet

- The Lifeline Illustration—a simple, visual way to share the Gospel

- John 3—Jesus' presentation to Nicodemus

- Your personal testimony

- The Roman Road—Scriptures from the book of Romans

- The message of the Cross

You may choose to utilize one of these or a combination of two or more of them. Of course, you may use any other approach that the Holy Spirit leads you to use.

Early one morning, David was having breakfast in the almost vacated downtown hotel restaurant before attending a company meeting. He was the first customer, so it was possible to have a fairly extended conversation with the waiter. The waiter, whose name tag read "Nasir," brought a menu and water to the table.

"Good morning, Nasir. You have an interesting name. Where are you from?" David began, employing the **FIRM** (Family, Interests, Religion, Message) conversation guide to open the way to share Jesus with him.

Nasir smiled. "Good morning. I am from Bangladesh."

"Bangladesh must be an interesting country, but I've never been there. Tell me about it."

Obviously pleased to find someone with an interest in his homeland, Nasir delightedly shared some details about the country, his family, and himself. He was an engineer who had come to the USA to work and was employed in the restaurant while getting established in his profession. He indicated that he now lived in a suburban area named Sugar Creek.

"Oh, I know that area," David replied, picking up on this opportunity to establish a common bond with Nasir. "Tell me more about yourself, your family, your religious background . . ."

"Oh, I am married, my wife is here with me, but most of my family is in Bangladesh. And I am Muslim," Nasir said.

"Then I'm sure you know about Jesus. Muslims call Him Esa. Isn't that right?" David probed.

"Yes, it is. We believe that he was a prophet."

"Nasir, the Bible teaches that Jesus is the Son of God. I have come to know Him as my personal Savior. He changed my life. May I share with you how you can know Him, be forgiven of your sins, and know that you have eternal life?" David asked. "I'll use this napkin and my pen to illustrate." (David had decided to use the Lifeline Illustration.)

"Romans 3:9 indicates that all humanity is under sin," David went on. "As I hold the napkin here, we will let it represent the barrier of sin that stands between humanity and God. As I place my pen beneath it, the pen represents the human race which is 'under' sin. As I place the pen over the napkin, it represents God who is holy and above sin. All of us have a capacity and a yearning for God, yet we have a prideful sin nature that causes us to resist God and attempt to reach Him through our own efforts." (David moved the pen, which was under the napkin, upward, illustrating the attempt of humanity to penetrate the sin barrier and try to reach God.) "But it is impossible! Sinful humanity cannot make its own way to God. The sin barrier is impenetrable.

"God intervened to do what no human could do. He came in and through the person of Jesus Christ to penetrate the sin barrier. He came into our situation and lived a sinless life." David penetrated the napkin with his pen until it formed the shape of a cross. "Then Jesus was crucified, bearing our sins in His own body on the cross. He became the lifeline from God to us. He is the only way we can have life. He made the way to bring us through the sin barrier by coming to Him and receiving Him. Does this make sense to you?"

Nasir nodded slowly. "Yes . . . but I believe in one god, Allah. You have spoken of *two* gods."

"No, Nasir, I am sharing with you about one God. There is one God who has manifested Himself as three Persons—Father, Son, and Holy Spirit. Let me give you an illustration. It is very inadequate to explain such a great spiritual truth, but, I am one man, and at the same time I am a son to my mother, a husband to my wife, and a father to my daughter."

David sensed the inadequacy of the illustration and began to explain further, but Nasir interrupted. He slapped the table with his hand and said, "Yes, that's it! I understand! It is wonderful!"

It seemed almost too good to be true. The Holy Spirit took this completely inadequate explanation and used it to give Nasir faith in Jesus as the Son of God. David hurried on, pressing for a decision. "Nasir, are you ready to believe in Jesus as the Son of God who died for your sins?"

"Yes, I am!"

"Will you accept Him as your Savior and Lord? Will you pray with me now and ask Him to forgive you of your sins and be your Savior?" David asked.

Standing there beside the table, Nasir bowed his head

and prayed, trusting Christ as His own Savior and Lord. Both Nasir and David praised God together.

When David finished breakfast, he asked for the check. Nasir refused to bring one. "I want to take care of it!" he insisted. "After all you have done for me in helping me know Jesus, I must do something for you."

Step 3: Ask the Person to Receive Christ

Asking a person to trust Christ is a critical point in the witnessing encounter.

Your goal in sharing, of course, is to lead the person to a genuine experience of conversion and salvation. It is possible for the person to make a premature decision that will give him or her a false sense of spiritual security. Pressuring people into insincere decisions will become a barrier to their salvation. Let the Holy Spirit draw the person to Christ according to His schedule, not yours. Cooperate with the Holy Spirit as you share. He will help you realize if the person has come to the point of being spiritually prepared to trust Him. Trusting Christ is a matter of the will. You can ask a person to do so. You can continue to discuss and share, but you cannot force another person to trust Him. If there is continued resistance, it is usually best to conclude the conversation leaving the door open to share another time.

Be aware that Satan is likely to attack at this point, and you will be engaged in spiritual warfare. Satan won't be happy about losing someone over which he has dominion. He may attempt to disrupt the sharing conversation by stimulating distractions. A telephone will ring. The baby will begin to cry. The dog will start to bark. Someone will come to the door. You can just depend on it. As one Christian approached this point in sharing Christ, the person he was sharing with received one phone call after another. The

Christian had to begin again three times before the person finally received Christ.

If an interruption does occur, courteously and as quickly as possible get back to the point of asking him or her to receive Christ. You may need to review the main points you have presented before asking again.

Satan may attempt to intimidate you as a witness, suggesting thoughts of fear of rejection and uncertainty. By faith, banish each of these self-centered thoughts. Satan may also try to plant suggestions that this may not be the right time. Be sensitive to the Holy Spirit and proceed, trusting Him moment by moment.

Realize that many people do not receive Christ because no one asks them. Don't be hesitant to ask. Trust God to give the wisdom to deal with the response that comes.

It is best to ask the person to receive Christ in a way that is natural and comfortable to you. Ask in a way that places pressure on you rather than the person to whom you are witnessing. You may use "I" statements such as "I would like to pray with you as you receive Christ," or "It would be a joy for me to pray with you as you receive Christ." These are much less threatening than "will you" questions, such as "Will you accept Christ now?"

Try one of these approaches:

- "May I ask you a question? Is there any good reason why you could not receive Christ now?" (Allow time for an answer.) Usually having come to this point in sharing the Gospel, the person will respond by saying something like, "No, there is no good reason for me not to trust Christ now." "Then you may express your faith in Him through prayer by calling on Him now. It would be a joy for me to pray with you and for you, then you pray and ask Him to come into your heart. There is nothing magical about prayer. It is the expression of your faith in

Christ. Romans 10:13–14 says, 'For whoever calls on the name shall be saved. How then shall they call on Him in whom they have not believed?' May we do that now?" If, on the other hand, the person says there is a reason they could not trust Christ, then you may ask, "What seems to be standing in the way?"

- "If I could, I would do this for you, but I cannot. You have to do it yourself. But I can pray with you as you call on the Lord. Could we do that now?"

Step 4: Lead the Person to Pray

If you are using an evangelistic booklet or the *People Sharing Jesus* New Testament, don't forget to use the suggested prayers you'll find in these tools because they'll be a great help at this important step.

The time of prayer is a very tender moment. Do not rush it. There are many mistaken concepts about prayer. Some people do not know what prayer is or how to pray. It might help to say, "You can receive Jesus through prayer. Praying is talking to God from your heart as you would talk to another person."

Others are afraid to pray. They are afraid they may not know what to say. You will need to direct their prayer.

I'll never forget the time I witnessed to Bill. He was a construction worker in the Midwest. His twelve-year-old daughter, Cindy, had trusted Christ as Savior and Lord. She asked me to share Jesus with her father. He was cordial and interested as we conversed about his life, interests, and relationship with Christ. Both the Gospel and Cindy's concern touched his heart. But when we came to the point of prayer, Bill said, "I can't pray! I ain't never prayed before in my life." The Holy Spirit led me to respond, "Bill, could we talk to God about your not being able to pray?" I asked God to help him. Then I asked Bill to talk to God about not being able to pray. What happened next was a marvelous work of the Spirit.

Bill began to talk to God. "God," he said, "you know I ain't never prayed in my life. Please help me to pray." As he paused, I said, "Now, Bill, you are praying. Ask God to forgive your sins. Ask Christ to come into your heart." The man who could not pray began to pray and received Christ as the Holy Spirit drew him.

You may have to instruct the person in what to say in prayer. Suggest, "If you can mean it and these words express what you want to say, you might pray something like this: Lord Jesus, thank You for dying for me on the cross. I know that I'm a sinner. I repent of my sins. Please forgive my sins. I do believe in You. I receive You now as my Savior and Lord. Come into my heart and help me to live like You want me to live. Thank You for coming into my heart."

When you ask people to pray to receive Christ, there will be various responses.

Following are five possible responses and suggestions of how to deal with them. The person may:

- **Pray aloud immediately.**
  Although praying aloud is not necessary for salvation, it will help to give the new Christian assurance. Verbalizing the prayer expressing repentance and faith will reinforce the vividness of the memory of the person's experience of trusting Jesus. It will help in recalling a definite time of consciously placing faith and trust in Jesus Christ as Savior and Lord. If he or she does pray aloud, lead the person to confess Christ as Savior and Lord. Then give instruction about how to begin the Christian life.

169

- **Say nothing.**
  If the person says nothing, wait! At a time like this, a minute will feel like an hour. Pray silently! Realize that a struggle is going on in the person's heart and mind. God is at work. Do not become anxious. Allow time for the struggle of commitment. It's biblical to count the cost, and there is a high cost involved in accepting the free gift of eternal life.

  As my wife and I shared Jesus with a young woman, we asked her to pray. She was silent for what seemed to us an eternity. After she prayed and trusted Christ, she revealed the reason for her lengthy silence. She was living with a man who was not her husband. To trust Christ would mean making an immediate change in that relationship.

  After waiting for an appropriate length of time, you may ask again, "Jesus is standing at the door of your heart. He will come in if you invite Him. Won't you ask Him to come in now?"

- **Pray silently.**
  The person may be so timid about prayer that he or she cannot pray aloud. Explain that God hears the prayer of the heart. Repeat the words that may be said to the Father. Ask the person to call on the Lord silently. Wait. Then ask, "If you did pray and are receiving Christ, please take my hand and say, 'I am receiving Christ.'" Guide the person to assurance of salvation and give instruction in beginning the Christian life.

- **Repeat after you as you verbalize the prayer.**
  You may sense that the person is having difficulty formulating a prayer. If the Holy Spirit leads, you may say, "If it would help, I can say the prayer. If

170

the words express the desire of your heart, you can pray after me." If the person repeats the prayer, ask, "If you are receiving Christ and committing your life to Him, please take my hand and say, 'I will!'" Guide the person to assurance of salvation and give instruction in how to begin the Christian life.

- **Refuse to pray and trust Christ.**
  If the person hesitates, you may discuss the reluctance to pray and trust Christ. Ask if you may pray instead. After a time of prayer, the person may be open to trust Christ. If he or she continues to resist, do your best to leave the door open.

  You may say, "I understand. There was a time in my life when I felt the same way. It's the most important decision you'll ever make. But I feel that you are interested. The Holy Spirit will continue to speak to your heart. May I leave you some literature (a witnessing booklet, tract, or New Testament) for you to read? Please feel free to call me. I pray that we'll have an opportunity to talk again soon."

Step 5: Guide into Assurance

It is important to immediately guide the new believer to assurance of salvation in Christ.

First, solidify the commitment. One way to do this is to give opportunity for a verbal expression of commitment. In asking for a confession of faith, you may say, "If you are receiving Christ now and committing your life to Him, please take my hand and say, 'I will.'"

This will help the new Christian nail down the time and reality of his or her commitment. I have had the joy of observing many new Christians break into a radiant smile as they squeezed my hand and said, "I will." In times of difficulty and doubt, they will be able to look back and remember the moment Jesus came into their lives.

Ask the new believer to thank God in prayer for His salvation. Give him or her an opportunity to pray, then you can pray and give thanks to the Lord. If someone is nearby, introduce the new Christian to them. Ask the new Christian to share what has just happened. You may need to assist him or her in telling about the experience. Rejoice together.

Stepping onto an elevator, Duane stood face to face with a dejected-looking young man whose nametag read "Luke." "Good morning, Luke," Duane said. "How is your day?"

"Not so good. I'm having a rough day."

Duane was quick to respond, "Luke, may I share with you how you can have a better day every day? This little booklet will tell you how it can happen." Duane handed Luke a Gospel booklet that clearly told how to accept Christ and experience salvation.

Luke received the booklet with interest and began to leaf through it. He stepped off the elevator with Duane and in a few minutes had received the Lord. Duane asked him to go to his room and meet his wife. When he had introduced them, Duane asked Luke to share what had just happened in his life.

Luke excitedly said, "I've just trusted Christ! God sent this man to me. This is what I've been needing!"

He had the joy of confessing Christ, and together they shared the promises from the Bible to give assurance and instruction.

Second, share Bible promises about salvation. If you are using a witnessing booklet or the *People Sharing Jesus* New Testament, refer to the "Guide to Assurance" in that tool, or use the following verses. These will help to give the new believer the assurance of salvation.

The Holy Spirit gives assurance to the heart and mind of a believer through the promises of the Word of God. As a person turns from sin in repentance to God and trusts Jesus Christ as Savior and Lord, God gives assurance to the new believer as His child. "The Spirit Himself bears witness with our spirit that we are children of God" (Rom. 8:16 NKJV).

- **Read Revelation 3:20:** "Behold, I stand at the door and knock. If anyone hears My voice and opens the door, I will come in to him and dine with him, and he with Me" (NKJV). Explain that Jesus has promised to come into any life that will open the door for Him to do so.

  Ask: "Did you open the door of your life for Him to come in? If so, where is He now?"

  Answer: "He is in my life!"

- **Read John 5:24:** "Most assuredly, I say to you, he who hears My word and believes in Him who sent Me has everlasting life, and shall not come into judgment, but has passed from death into life" (NKJV).

  Ask: "Did you hear His Word and believe?"

  Answer: "Yes I did."

  Ask: "On the basis of this promise, what do you have?"

  Answer: "Everlasting life."

Ask: "What promise does Jesus give about your future?"

Answer: "I will not come into judgment."

Ask: "What does Jesus say you have experienced?"

Answer: "I have passed from death into life."

- **Read Romans 10:13:** "For whoever calls upon the name of the Lord shall be saved" (NKJV).

  Ask: "What does this promise say about you?"

  Answer: "I am saved!"

- **Read 1 John 5:11–13:** "And this is the testimony: that God has given us eternal life, and this life is in His Son. He who has the Son has life; he who does not have the Son of God does not have life. These things I have written to you who believe in the name of the Son of God, that you may know that you have eternal life, and that you may continue to believe in the name of the Son of God" (NKJV).

  Ask: "According to this promise, what has God given you?"

  Answer: "He has given me eternal life."

  Ask: "This verse says 'He who has the Son has life.' Because of this, how do you know you have life?"

  Answer: "Because I have Jesus."

Now ask the new believer to pray and give thanks to God for His wonderful salvation.

Step 6: Instruct the New Believer

The responsibility of the person sharing Jesus does not end when the unbeliever prays to receive Christ. Helping a new Christian grow is both a wonderful privilege as well as a responsibility. The new babe in Christ needs your instruction. Because you have led him or her to Christ, you have a relationship and an opportunity to give guidance that no one else may have. When a baby is born, the parents and pediatrician do not pitch it out on the sidewalk and say, "Okay, kid! You are born. Now go live it." Not at all! They love the baby. They know it needs care, nurture, food, and instruction to grow. Just so, the new child in Christ needs love, a supportive fellowship, prayer, and the spiritual nurture and food of the Word of God. Guide the new Christian in the basic essentials for growth and obedience to Christ. Again, if you are using the *People Sharing Jesus* New Testament or an evangelistic booklet, use the "Basic Follow-Up" in that tool, or you can use the following verses:

- **Public profession of faith** (Matt. 10:32–33). Jesus has called each of His followers to take an open and public stand for Him. Doing so makes the decision to trust and follow Christ definite and clear cut. It declares the Christian's accountability to live for Christ.

- **Baptism and church membership** (Acts 2:38–42). Instruct the new believer about the need for baptism and the supporting fellowship of a caring, Christ-centered, Bible-believing church. Baptism is the outward expression of an inner faith in Christ. It identifies the believer as being one with Christ and with other believers. This unity is expressed by becoming an active part of a local church fellowship.

- **Intimate communion with God through confession of sin** (1 Thess. 5:17 and 1 John 1:9). Prayer is like spiritual breathing. It gives vitality to the spiritual life. When sin happens in a life, instantaneous confession brings cleansing, refreshing renewal.

- **Spiritual nurture and guidance** (1 Peter 2:2). The food for the Christian life is the Word of God. It is like milk for the babe in Christ and meat for the mature Christian.

- **Witness for Christ** (Acts 1:8). Explain that witnessing is sharing with others what Christ has done in one's life. Sharing Jesus is His assignment to every Christian.

Help the new Christian get started in Bible study and church attendance. Volunteer to meet the person at church on Sunday or, even better, arrange to pick him or her up to go with you.

But what if the person does not accept Christ? How do you conclude the conversation and visit?

Stay positive. Remember that although the person did not accept Christ, you have sown the seed of Christ's love. The Holy Spirit is doing His work. You can sense the approval of the Holy Spirit, for, remember, success in sharing is sharing Jesus in the power of the Holy Spirit and leaving the results with God.

If at any point in the conversation and presentation of the Gospel the person indicates unwillingness for you to share further, honor that wish, but be sure to leave the door open.

Be courteous. Treat the person as you would want to be treated. To close the conversation, consider saying the following:

- "You have been gracious to permit me to share with you. Thank you so much. May we share again sometime?"

- "I understand how you feel. But somewhere deep down, I sense that you are interested in the Lord and His way for you. May I leave some biblical material for you to read? It contains ideas that you may want to explore further."

- "I appreciate your allowing me to share with you about Christ. He means so much to me." (At this point you may share your one-and-a-half-minute testimony. Make sure it is brief or you risk losing the interest of the person.)

- "Thank you for talking with me. The church I attend is a great place to explore the Bible and the claims of Christ. May I invite you to be my guest on Sunday?"

- "I sense you have an interest in God's Word. May I invite you to attend a Bible study with me?" Or "There is an interesting Bible study you may want to attend."

Step 7: Follow Up

Follow-up is a key to helping the new Christian grow.

- Pray daily for him or her.

- Invite the new Christian to accompany you to your church or help him or her locate and get started in another church.

- Make periodic follow-up contacts for encouragement and assistance.

- Provide beginning Bible study material, like a *People Sharing Jesus* New Testament, or help the person join a new Christians' class or a discipleship group.

- If possible, take him or her with you to share Jesus with someone else.

If the new Christian lives too far away for you to follow up, attempt to locate someone in his or her area who will do so.

These steps in sharing Jesus are not intended to be rigid guidelines to adhere to; rather, they are intended to help you think through the possibilities of what you can do and say in the process of presenting the Gospel. The more you share Jesus, the more comfortable you will be in sharing. As the Holy Spirit leads, you will develop your own style of witnessing. Continue to pray daily that God will give you divine appointments. Keep on sowing the seed of the Gospel, and God will give the harvest.

Chapter Ten: Personal Review Questions

1. As you follow the leading of the Holy Spirit, how would you develop a relationship which would open the opportunity to share Jesus?

2. Which of the eight methods for presenting the Gospel right now best fits into your style and approach to ministry? What appeals to you about this method?

3. What are some of the positive responses you might expect when you graciously and clearly give another person the opportunity to receive Jesus? Compare the best-case scenarios; even the worst case just closes the door for right now.

4. How could you help the new believer understand the simplicity of prayer?

5. How does the Christian *know* he/she has eternal life?

6. Using the analogy of the newborn baby from 1 Peter 2:1, how would you help a baby Christian to begin growing in his/her faith?

7. Continuing to use the analogy from 1 Peter, explain why follow-up is essential for the new believer.

Chapter 11

Understand How to Share the Word in Witness

The greatest privilege a person can have is to lead someone to the Savior. You will make a friend for life and for eternity when you do. You will experience the wonderful joy of a special fellowship with the Lord. It will be like one Christian excitedly said after leading a friend to Christ, "I felt like I was experiencing Christ for the first time all over again myself."

In this chapter you will learn several powerful methods that will help you share Jesus naturally, comfortably, and successfully. By being familiar with how to use several approaches, you will have the tools to share Christ with different people at the point of their need and in a way they can best relate to. It will also give you the optional approaches that best fit your own unique personality and giftedness. I want to give you four powerful tools for sharing Jesus in this chapter. The first is easier—the booklet approach. The second is the Lifeline Illustration. The third is the great evangelistic conversation of Jesus with Nicodemus—John 3. The fourth is the one where you are the expert and authority—How to Share Your Personal Testimony. The Lifeline Illustration, as you recall, is in Step 2 of Chapter 10.

An Appendix has been included in the book that contains

several other approaches for sharing Christ. It includes an exciting way parents, grandparents, Bible teachers, and friends can share Jesus with children, *How to Use the Message of the Cross, How to Use the Roman Road, How to Share Jesus with a Person Who Does Not Believe in God,* and *How to Use Life's Great Questions to Share Christ.* The *People Sharing Jesus* New Testament also has an outline of marked Scriptures and comments that will help you share clearly how a person can come to Christ.

How to Use an Evangelistic Booklet

For many years, evangelistic booklets have been used by Christians to present the plan of salvation. In fact, multitudes have come to Christ through these booklets. It's a good idea to always have one or two with you to share with another or simply to leave.

Advantages to Using an Evangelistic Booklet

There are several advantages to using a witnessing booklet to share Jesus:

- **A booklet is simple to use.** Anyone who can read can easily use an evangelistic booklet to lead people to Christ. Jason stopped by for a quick hamburger at a fast-food place. Lisa took his order. It was late and other customers were not coming in. Jason began to converse with Lisa using the **FIRM** (Family, Interests, Religion, Message) conversation guide. Lisa expressed an interest in Jesus, saying that she was "in the process of considering coming to Christ." Jason asked her to read through a Gospel booklet with him. Lisa tearfully prayed and trusted

Jesus. Then she asked Jason to share with her sister who was working in the back. But her sister was busy with her work and could not get free to meet Jason. Jason promised to return the next night to talk to her. The next night when Jason returned, he was greeted by a joyful Lisa. Lisa told him that he would not need to talk to her sister. She said, "I took the booklet you left with me and did with my sister what you did with me. She trusted Christ and now both of us are Christians." Jason, Lisa, and her sister did share together with excitement and joy about how to follow Christ as His disciples.

- **A booklet illustrates the Gospel** as well as gives the Scriptures and explanation of how to receive Christ. The diagrams and illustrations are excellent tools aiding understanding.

- **A booklet can be left with the person** with whom you have shared Jesus.

- **Training Christians to use the booklets can be done quickly and easily.** As a pastor I used a different booklet to train our church members on Sunday morning periodically. I did this about once a year instead of the sermon. It always resulted in believers being equipped to share and in some lost people trusting Christ. I always explained that I had two objectives: First, to share Jesus so that any person present may understand and receive Him during that service. Each time we did so, someone received Christ. One Sunday, a medical doctor who had been attending our church came forward and said, "When you came to the prayer in the booklet, I prayed and received Christ."

My second objective was to train each Christian to read through the booklet with someone else and lead the person to Christ. I would explain that during the week at work, at school, in the neighborhood, or with a family member or friend, all of us will likely have a "divine appointment" and can share Jesus if we are sensitive to the person and to the Holy Spirit. From the brief time of simply going through the booklet on Sunday morning, Brandon used it to lead an acquaintance to Jesus the very next week.

The booklet is an excellent tool to use in marketplace evangelism. It can be used during lunch hour, break time, or before or after work.

Witnessing Products Available

Many excellent evangelistic booklets are available today. Some pastors and churches have developed and printed their own to use in their particular context. Several evangelists have designed effective booklets. Every time we had an evangelist minister in our church, we asked him to teach our people how to use his particular approach and materials to share Jesus.

Some effective booklets available for purchase are:

"Eternal Life," Home Mission Board, SBC, 1350 Spring St. NW, Atlanta, GA 30367–5601. Customer Services: 1–800–634–2462, or fax 1–800–253–2823. *I like to use the "Eternal Life" booklet with those who are less familiar with the Gospel. It is more thorough than some. It is especially good to leave with a person or to mail to them, along with a letter, for private study.*

"Four Spiritual Laws," Campus Crusade for Christ International, Arrowhead Springs, 38–00, San Bernardino, CA 92414. *"Four Spiritual Laws" is the first booklet I ever used. I like it because of its orderly arrangement and thought pattern. Its illustrations are powerful. A person who thinks very logically will appreciate it. I often introduce it by saying, "This booklet has been used extensively on college campuses."*

"Here's Hope," Home Mission Board, SBC, 1350 Spring St. NW, Atlanta, GA 30367–5601. Customer Services: 1–800–634–2462, or fax 1–800–253–2823. *"Here's Hope" is contemporary and powerful. As it is shared, it captivates the attention of the reader and hearer. It lends itself to creativity in introducing and presenting it. It is excellent in giving guidance for what to do after a person has prayed and trusted Christ.*

"How to Have a Full and Meaningful Life," Sunday School Board, 127 Ninth Ave. N., Nashville, TN 37234. Call: 1–800–458–BSSB. *This booklet is very useful not only for its content but for its name and emphasis. The name is contemporary and especially appeals to those into New Age thinking.*

"Steps to Peace with God," Billy Graham Evangelistic Association, Box 779, Minneapolis, MN 55440. Call: 1–800–487–0433 for churches; (612) 338–0500 for individual orders. *The name recognition and respect many have for its author, Billy Graham, usually gives an immediate opening to share it. Most people are interested in and want to have the booklet written by Billy Graham.*

"A Woman's Search for Self-Fulfillment," Home Mission Board, SBC, 1350 Spring St. NW, Atlanta, GA 30367–5601. Customer Services: 1–800–634–2462. *This booklet captivates the interest of many women. It is especially good to leave with a woman for her study later. My wife Kathy uses it often.*

Procedures for Sharing Jesus

- Use the conversation guide **FIRM** (Friends, Interests, Religion, Message) in Chapter 4 to begin the witness conversation.

- Present the message. Begin by introducing the booklet. Here are some examples of how you can introduce the booklet in varied and creative ways:

"I have a booklet that has come to mean much to me. May I share it with you?"

"May I share with you a booklet that explains how you can know for certain that you have eternal life?"

"This booklet has a wonderful message about how to have a full and meaningful life. May I share it with you?"

If you are using "Steps to Peace with God," you might say, "I'm sure you've heard of Billy Graham. May I share with you a booklet he wrote that shows how you can have peace with God and eternal life?"

In witnessing to a woman using "A Woman's Search for Self-Fulfillment," you might say, "This is a booklet especially for women. May I share it with you?"

- Read through the booklet together. Ask the person to whom you are witnessing to hold one side of the booklet while you hold the other.

- Use a pencil or your finger as a pointer to direct attention.

- Keep the person's attention by involving him or her. Ask nonthreatening questions periodically to involve the person. Ask the person to read some of the verses aloud rather than your reading them yourself. Reading the verse aloud utilizes the senses of sight, speech, and hearing to impress the Scripture more strongly on the mind of the person with whom you are sharing.

- Be sure to give the opportunity to pray the prayer

to receive Christ and make a personal commitment to Him

- Share the assurance and follow-up material in the last part of the booklet, whether or not the person has accepted Christ. You may say, "Here are some important things you will need to know when you do receive Christ." God may use the follow-up material to help the person better understand that salvation is by grace through faith.

Practice Sharing Jesus

Practice sharing the booklet with someone. Read through it with a family member or friend. Ask him or her to play the role of the unbeliever. You may even ask an unbeliever to allow you to practice with him or her. Some have been led to Christ while practicing.

Personally, I like to have three or four different booklets in my pocket at all times. I have found that each booklet has some distinctive strengths and appeals to people of different types of personalities or backgrounds.

Remember! There is no bad method for leading people to Christ. God uses all types of approaches to reach all types of people.

How to Use the Lifeline Illustration

Illustrating what God has done to effect our salvation is a powerful tool in presenting the plan of salvation. It can help people understand by visualizing as well as hearing the Gospel. I have used this simple demonstration many times in leading people to Christ.

The illustration may be presented, using a pen or pencil

and a piece of paper, napkin, or lightweight card. If these are not available, you may use your hands.

Presentation:

Ask, "May I share with you about how to come to know Christ as your Savior? I can demonstrate, using my pen and this piece of paper.

"All humanity is 'under sin'" (Rom. 3:9 NKJV). As an illustration, the paper will represent sin. If I place my pen _under_ the paper, we can easily see that humankind is under sin.

"On the other hand, God is holy. When I place my pen _above_ the paper, it represents God's position with regard to sin. God is above sin.

Holy God

Sin Barrier

Sinful Humanity

"One who has sinned may attempt to reach God." (Using your pen to represent sinful people, move it up toward God. It will collide with the paper representing the sin barrier.) "Sinful people attempt to reach God in many ways. These may include good works, reformation, morality, religious performance, and philanthropy. But it is impossible for one who has sinned to reach holy God in these ways.

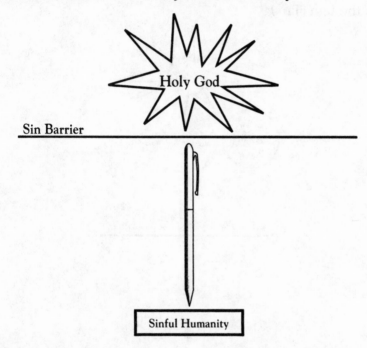

"The only possibility for sinful people to break through the sin barrier and receive life from God is for God to intervene in the human situation. Under sin, we are spiritually dead. God is the only source of spiritual life. Jesus Christ is the 'way, the truth, and the life' (John 14:6). _He is the only lifeline to God._

"God did what human beings could never do! In the person of Jesus Christ, His Son, God came into the human situation. He penetrated the sin barrier to live a sinless life on earth. On the cross, He died as He paid the price for our sins. There He 'bore our sins in His own body' (1 Peter 2:24 NKJV), providing the way for sinful people to come to God."

(Penetrate the paper with your pen. It will form a cross, representing Jesus dying for our sins to be "the way, the truth, and the life." Sinful people can now come to God through Him.)

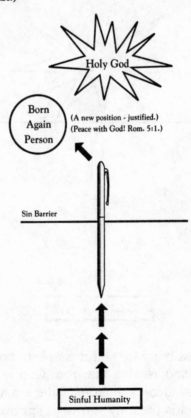

Sinful people, through repentance and faith, come to Christ, are forgiven, and become children of God. (Acts 20:21)

"You can receive the gift of salvation by repenting (turning from your sin and self-efforts) and by faith coming to Christ. You must trust Him as your Savior and Lord. You will be born again as a child of God. You will have a new position of being made right with God. You will have peace with God and begin your new life on your way to heaven."

How to Use John 3

John 3:1–18 is an exciting, simple-to-use way to share Jesus. As you use John 3 to share Jesus, I am sure that you, like many others, will sense its power in helping unbelievers trust Christ. For several reasons it is highly effective in leading people to Christ.

Confidence Built by the Passage

- It is a single passage that can be used without skipping through several chapters and books that may give the appearance of using proof texts. By simply reading through it, a person can come to understand how to receive life through trusting Christ.

- It is a direct transcription of Jesus' words. It is Jesus Himself leading a man to conversion. His pattern and plan are the best anyone could follow.

- It is an excellent way to deal with excuses, problems, objections, and concerns before they arise. This is important. When people position themselves with an argument or excuse, they often feel bound to defend it because of human ego. It is better to deal with it scripturally before they position themselves.

Concerns Addressed by the Passage

Numerous concerns, questions, and problems are answered by Jesus in this passage. They can be shared as you sense that they are needed while you are reading through it together. If the unbeliever has a question or raises an objection, you may want to refer to one of these points:

- Jesus loves and is concerned for the individual (vv. 1–2, 16–17).

- Religion cannot save (vv. 1–3).

- Church membership cannot save (verses throughout passage).

- Morality, social, economic, or family position cannot save (vv. 1–5).

- Fear keeps people from Christ (v. 2).

- Conviction of sin opens people to Christ (v. 2).

- A person can receive the gift of salvation without having all the answers to spiritual questions (v. 6).

- Salvation is not by feeling, but by faith (vv. 14–15).

- Every person, regardless of his or her life situation, must experience the spiritual birth to become a child of God and go to heaven (vv. 3–5).

- There is only *one* way of salvation—through Jesus Christ. There are not *many* ways. There are not even *two* ways (v. 13).

- The death of Christ on the cross is necessary for the payment for sin (vv. 14–15).

- Everyone has been made for eternity. Each will live forever somewhere—in heaven with Christ, or in hell, separated from Him (v. 16).

- God has proven that He is for every person by giving His Son (v. 17).

- Spiritually, there are only two groups of people in the world—believers and unbelievers. There is no middle ground (v. 18).

Conversation Guide Through the Passage

The following is an example of a conversational approach in sharing John 3:1–18 (NKJV) with someone. I have personally used this approach many times. Responses usually are very natural and spontaneous. During a thirty-minute training period, I went through John 3:1–18 and explained how to use the following conversation guide with a group of Christians. Later that evening as we met for a share time, a young adult couple who had participated in the training reported that they had shared John 3 with three adults. All three accepted Christ!

I once shared John 3 with a brokenhearted father whose daughter had recently been killed in a tragic accident. Christian friends had been praying for Ed for years, but it took this incident for the Holy Spirit to prepare his heart for the Gospel. I went to his home to comfort him and his family. During the course of the visit, I read through John 3 with Ed and asked him to receive Christ. He responded to God's love, and his life was changed as he accepted Christ and became involved in the life of a local church.

In presenting the John 3 conversation guide, the one sharing is the **believer**. The believer has a divine appointment with an unbeliever who is called the **seeker**. Remember that a *divine appointment is when the path of a willing witness crosses the path of a seeker*. Unbelievers become seekers as the Holy Spirit convicts them of their sin and need and draws them to Christ. "God wants everyone to be saved" (1 Tim. 2:4). God uses the powerful team of three—the Word of God, the work of the Holy Spirit, and the witness of the believer—to bring people to Himself. The Holy Spirit is at work to help you share the Gospel with those with whom you have an opportunity.

During the conversation, you will want to involve the seeker in order to maintain his or her interest and to cooperate with the work of the Spirit as He draws the person to Christ. Ask the person to read a verse or part of a verse aloud. In a nonthreatening way, ask for comments from the seeker. "What does this verse mean to you personally?" Do not ask the person to interpret or give its meaning. Ask what it means personally to him or her.

Believer: "May I ask you a personal question?"

Seeker: "Yes, you may."

Believer: "Have you come to know Jesus Christ in a personal way, or would you say you are still in the process?"

Seeker: "I guess I am still in the process."

Believer: "Then you have given serious thought to it."

Seeker: "Yes, I've thought a lot about it lately."

Believer: "May I take a few minutes to share with you from the Bible how you can know for sure you have eternal life?"

"The greatest sermon ever preached, of course, was preached by Jesus. We usually think of great sermons being preached to a multitude of people. But the sermon in John 3 was given by Jesus to just one man in the middle of the night. Does that suggest anything to you?"

Seeker: "Yes. It suggests that Jesus cares for the individual."

Believer: "Let's read verse 1. (Read.) If you had lived next door to Nicodemus, you would have thought that he had it all. He appeared to be an ideal person. Yet, all of Nicodemus's fine qualities did not change the fact that he had a deep need. He was religious, a Pharisee. He was rich. He was respectable, a ruler. But none of these qualities filled the need of his heart. He saw in Jesus what he needed but did not have.

"Verse 2 says that Nicodemus came to Jesus at night. Why do you think he came in the night?"

Seeker: "He was probably afraid that others might see him."

Believer: "I think you're right. He was afraid of what others might say or do. Fear and peer pressure sometimes keep people from coming to Christ. It kept me from coming to Him for some time." (This would be a good time to share your own experience.) "Has that ever happened to you? Have you ever felt like that?"

Seeker: "Yes, I have." (Give the seeker an opportunity to express fear and deal with it.)

Believer: "There may have been another reason he came at night." (The purpose of this thought is to lead the seeker to realize his or her own sin.) "Nicodemus might have chosen this time because of his own conviction for sin. In the stillness of the night, with no distractions, he had to face the loneliness of his spiritual emptiness.

"When he came face to face with himself, he got up and came to Jesus. So as not to expose the superficiality of his spiritual life, he attempted to flatter Jesus by saying, 'Rabbi, we know that You are a teacher come from God; for no one can do these signs that You do unless God is with him.' Jesus brushed aside his compliment and got right to the point. He knew the heart of Nicodemus. John 2:25 says, 'and [he] had no need that anyone should testify of man, for He knew what was in man.'"

(At this point ask the seeker to read verse 3 aloud.) "Here is a verse where Jesus tells Nicodemus what is really important."

Seeker: "Jesus answered and said to him, 'Most assuredly, I say to you, unless one is born again, he cannot see the kingdom of God."

Believer: "What does this verse mean to you?" (Do not ask the seeker to interpret or give its meaning. Ask what it means *to him or her*.)

Seeker: "It means to me that you have to be born again."

Believer: "I remember the first time I heard about this, I didn't know what it meant. Do you understand this expression, or are you like I was?"

(Read verse 4.) "In verse 4, Nicodemus revealed his lack of understanding when he asked Jesus, 'How can a man be born when he is old? Can he enter the second time into his mother's womb and be born?' Nicodemus thought Jesus was speaking about the physical birth—reversing the process of nature and being born a second time. But in verses 5 and 6, Jesus corrects Nicodemus and tells him that He is speaking of a spiritual birth. Nicodemus's problem was that he equated his physical birth with salvation. He thought that because he had been born into a Jewish family and was a religious man, he was a child of God. Jesus reveals that to be born physically, one becomes a member of a human family. But to be a part of the family of God, one must be born spiritually."

(Read verse 5.) "In verse 5, Jesus speaks about being born of water. When some read this verse, they immediately think about baptism. Baptism is important, of course. But baptism does not save you from the consequences of your sins. When you commit your life to Christ, you will want to be baptized. However, this verse is not speaking about baptism. The water birth is the physical, or flesh, birth. Before a baby is born, it is encased in a bag of water in its mother's womb. The water breaks and the baby is born. The flesh, or water, birth is necessary for physical life. The spiritual birth is necessary for spiritual life and to be a child of God. You must have the inner change of a spiritual birth when you come to know Christ as your Savior." (You may choose to use this opportunity to explain the meaning of baptism.)

"At this point Nicodemus's eyes must have popped out on stems. In verse 7, Jesus said, 'Do not marvel that I said to you, You must be born again.' Then in verse 8, He used an illustration of the wind." (Ask the seeker to read the verse.) "How do we know the wind is blowing? We can't see it. We don't know where it comes from or where it is going."

Seeker: "You know the wind is blowing because you feel it and see the evidence of it."

Believer: "This is like being born of the Spirit. You can't see the Holy Spirit. You can't understand all the Spirit does. But you can feel His presence as He convicts you and draws you to Christ. And you can experience the changing work He does in your heart."

(Read verse 9.) "In verse 9, Nicodemus asked the question you or I would have asked: 'How can these things be?' In other words, 'How can this happen to me?' In verse 10, Jesus gently rebuked him, 'Are you the teacher of Israel, and do not know these things?' Then in verse 13, Jesus answered the question about how it can happen for you and me." (Ask the seeker to read the verse, or read it yourself.) "This verse indicates that the only one who can go to heaven is the One who came from heaven. Who would you say this is talking about?"

Seeker: "I guess it is talking about Jesus."

Believer: "Yes it is. The question is, 'If Jesus is the only

197

One who is qualified to go to heaven, then how can you and I go to heaven?"

Seeker: "The only way we can go to heaven is through Jesus."

Believer: (Read vv. 14–16.) "Right. The only way we can go to heaven is through the One who is going there, Jesus. In verses 14–16, Jesus explains how this can happen. He draws an illustration from the history of Israel. The people of Israel were in the wilderness. God miraculously provided food and water for them, but they continued to murmur and complain against the Lord. So God disciplined them by sending a plague of snakes into their camp. When the snakes began to bite the people and they died, Moses interceded in prayer. God told him to mold a snake out of brass and raise it up on a pole in the middle of the camp. Then when the people were bitten, they were to look to the brass snake on the pole and God would heal them. There was no magic in the brass snake. God healed as they responded by faith.

"Jesus applied this incident to His being lifted up on the cross. Whoever has been bitten by the serpent bite of sin will die spiritually. But if they will look to Him by faith, they will be forgiven of their sins and have eternal life. Then Jesus gave that beautiful promise, John 3:16: 'For God so loved the world that He gave His only begotten Son, that whoever believes in Him should not perish, but have everlasting life.'" (Ask the seeker to read verse 17.)

Seeker: "For God did not send His Son into the world to condemn the world, but that the world through Him might be saved."

Believer: "Jesus did not come to condemn you. He came to save you. Now let's read verse 18. This verse tells us that there are only two groups of people in the world as far as God is concerned. Note who they are and what God says about them: 'He who believes in Him is not condemned; but he who does not believe is condemned already, because he has not believed in the name of the only begotten Son of God.' Who are the two groups?"

Seeker: "Those who believe and those who do not believe."

Believer: "What does the verse say about the believer?"

Seeker: "The believer is not condemned."

Believer: "What about the unbeliever?"

Seeker: "The unbeliever is condemned already."

Believer: "Why does it say that the unbeliever is condemned already?"

Seeker: "Because he has not believed in Jesus."

Believer: "May I ask you a very personal question? I don't want to embarrass you. But in which of the two groups would you say you are right now?" (The seeker may respond in one of three ways: "I am a believer." "I am not a believer." "I do believe, but . . .")

Seeker 1: "I am a believer. I am not condemned."

Believer: "That's wonderful! When did you believe in Christ and receive Him?" (Give the seeker an opportunity to share his or her testimony of salvation and rejoice together.)

Seeker 2: "No, I am not a believer."

Believer: "Then may I share with you now about believing in Him? Will you believe now that Jesus is God's Son, that He died for your sins and will save you? Will you receive Him now?"

Seeker 3: "I do believe a lot of things about Jesus, but . . ."

Believer: "I think I understand what you're saying. Then, you do believe intellectually about Jesus, but you have not received Him personally into your life. Is that true?"

Seeker: "Yes, that is true."

Believer: "Let's read John 1:12. Notice two key words about becoming God's child. 'But as many as received Him, to them he gave the right to become children of God, even to those who believe in His name.' What are the two key words?"

Seeker: "They are *receive* and *believe*." (If the seeker has difficulty, share them with him or her.)

Believer: "If you truly believe in Christ, you will want to turn from your sin and receive Him as Lord and Savior. Now, because you believe, will you receive Him through prayer? I'll pray with you and for you as you call on Him. But my prayer will not make you a Christian. After I pray, call on Him in prayer yourself. He promised, 'Whoever calls on the name of the Lord shall be saved' (Rom. 10:13 NKJV)." (Lead the seeker to pray, then share God's promises of assurance and give instruction about following Christ. Don't forget the many helpful hints found in Chapter 10 of *People Sharing Jesus*.)

This conversation guide through John 3 is but one model for using the passage to share Christ. Of course, the seeker may give different responses and not follow this pattern at all. If so, you may discuss his or her responses and return to John 3 as quickly as possible. As long as you have mastered the main points of the passage listed on pages 92 and 93 you'll do great. You might even want to write them into your Bible so they'll be right there when you share. If the seeker appears to be going off on a tangent, you may courteously ask, "May we look back to what Jesus said in John 3? I believe it may answer some of your questions."

If the seeker is not open to receive Christ, ask him or her to read John 3 after you leave and consider praying privately to receive Christ. Courteously ask permission for an opportunity to visit at another time. Ask him or her to call you if you can be of help. Ask to have prayer before you go. Leave the door open for a follow-up visit.

How to Share Your Personal Testimony

To share Jesus effectively you need to tell *two stories*. First, *your story*—what Jesus has done for you. Second, *His story*—how Jesus can change the lives of others.

Your testimony is a powerful way to move into a presentation of the Gospel and to encourage a person to trust Jesus. It will immediately secure the attention of the listener and help you share with confidence because you are the authority on what happened to you. John powerfully shared his personal encounter with Jesus to introduce the Gospel to us when he wrote 1 John:

> That which was from the beginning, which we have heard, which we have seen with our eyes, which we have looked at and our hands have touched—this we proclaim concerning the Word of life. The life appeared; we have seen it and testify to it, and we proclaim to you the eternal life, which was with the Father and has appeared to us. *We proclaim to you what we have seen and heard*, so that you also may have fellowship with us. And our fellowship is with the Father and with his Son, Jesus Christ. (1 John 1:1–3 NIV, italics added)

The Power of Your Personal Testimony

John was not the only one who shared his personal testimony. Paul had been arrested and rescued from the violent crowd that sought to kill him in the temple. In presenting his defense and sharing the Gospel, he gave them his personal testimony with power (Acts 22:1–21). He gave his testimony again when he was brought to trial before King Agrippa (Acts 26). Agrippa and those present were moved by the power of God through Paul's witness.

In John 4, Jesus met a Samaritan woman at Jacob's well.

He began the conversation by putting Himself at her disposal. He asked her for a drink of water. Then He told her that if she asked Him, He would give her living water. Her interest was captivated. As she asked for the water that would cause her never to thirst again, Jesus told her to go bring her husband. She replied that she had no husband. Jesus told her that she spoke the truth—she had had five husbands and now was living with a man who was not her husband. Then Jesus revealed to her who He was. After their discussion, the woman went back to her hometown and told her neighbors what had happened. "Come, see a man who told me everything I ever did. Could this be the Christ?" (v. 29 NIV). "And many of the Samaritans of that city believed in Him because of the word of the woman who testified, 'He told me all that I ever did'" (John 4:39, NKJV).

In John 9, Jesus healed a blind man. The Pharisees, desiring to find fault with Jesus, interrogated the man who had received his sight. His response was a simple testimony of what Jesus had done for him. "One thing I do know. I was blind but now I see!" (v. 25 NIV).

- Like every Christian, you have a powerful testimony to share. You have had the experience of salvation through Christ. The power of God will accompany the sharing of your experience.

- Like every testimony, your testimony is both unique and interesting. There is no other testimony exactly like yours. God will use the uniqueness of your testimony to touch lives in a way that no other can touch them. God wants to use all the different testimonies of His people to reach all types of people.

- Your personal testimony will catch the attention of the unbeliever. People are interested in what has happened to other people. The advertising industry has capitalized on the effectiveness of using personal-interest stories.

- Your personal testimony will establish empathy, helping the person see himself or herself in a similar situation to yours. It will help people realize that they, too, can experience the Lord Jesus.

- A personal testimony is difficult to refute. The experience has happened to you. You are a specialist on your own story. The antagonistic Pharisees had no defense for the simple, forthright testimony of the blind man who had been healed.

Preparing Your Personal Testimony

You may use one of two types of personal testimonies:

- A *salvation testimony* is the story of how you became a Christian.

- A *recovery testimony* is the story of how Jesus helped you at a point of need in your life.

Successful, powerful salvation and recovery testimonies have several elements that you'll want to incorporate:

My Salvation Testimony

1. My life before receiving Christ

2. How I received Jesus Christ

3. How Jesus Christ makes my life meaningful

My Recovery Testimony

1. My life seemed fairly normal until . . .

2. I discovered hope and help in Jesus when . . .

3. I am glad I have a personal relationship with Jesus today because . . .

Once you've shared your testimony, you can ask, "May I share with you how something like this can happen to you?"

- Give adequate and precise details showing how Christ became Savior and Lord of your life. Tell about yourself. Humor and human interest are keys. Most of us find that human interest is easier to achieve than humor. The average unbeliever thinks a Christian comes from another world or is strange and unusual. Be sure *not* to leave the impression that walking down an aisle, joining a church, or being baptized is what made you a Christian! Turning from your sins to Christ and placing your faith in Him is what did it. As important as these acts of obedience to Christ are, they did not provide forgiveness and eternal life and will not do so for anyone else!

- Be sure that in your testimony you clearly show the person how to receive the gift of salvation.

- Use language that the non-Christian can understand (1 Cor. 14:9). Avoid churchy, religious, theological terms. You understand them, but the other person may not. Such terms as "walked the aisle," "took the preacher's hand," "justified," "convicted," and "redeemed" may be meaningless or even misleading.

- When useful, relate your testimony to Bible verses. Your experience will illustrate the Bible truth.

- Bring your testimony up-to-date by sharing what Jesus means to you today.

- Make your testimony brief—no longer than a minute and a half.

In Ian Fleming's _From Russia with Love_, James Bond's friend captures the enemy. He ties the villain up in a chair to hold him for a few hours while Bond rescues the leading lady. Bond's friend settles in for a bit of mischievous "torture" by saying, "I have led a fascinating life. Let me tell you _all_ about it."

It is not realistic to assume that the person you are witnessing to will want to hear everything about your life. It may be that they need to tell you their own story. Prepare your testimony so that you can share it in about a minute and a half. Get to the point quickly, realizing that the attention span of the listener may be brief.

Practice Sharing Your Personal Testimony

- Write out your testimony, using the three-point outline. Practice reading it aloud several times.

- Ask a person you know to allow you to share it with him or her.

- Ask God to guide you to a person with whom you can share.

- Introduce your testimony by saying, "May I share with you the most wonderful thing that ever happened to me? It changed my life!"

- In concluding your testimony, ask, "Has this kind of experience happened to you?"

Below is a sample worksheet for preparing your personal testimony.

MY SALVATION TESTIMONY

"May I share with you the most wonderful thing that has ever happened to me?"

1. My life before receiving Christ:

2. How I received Jesus Christ:

3. How Jesus Christ makes my life meaningful:

"May I share with you how something like this can happen in your life?"

MY RECOVERY TESTIMONY

"May I share with you something that means so much to me?"

1. My life seemed fairly normal until . . .

2. I discovered hope and help in Jesus when . . .

3. I am glad I have a personal relationship with Jesus today because . . .

"May I share how something like this can happen to you?"

The following is the actual *salvation testimony* of Jennie Hitt.

"May I share with you the most wonderful thing that has ever happened to me?"

(Jennie first tells of 1. *Her life before she received Christ.*)

"My life was filled with fear daily from childhood until I was twenty-nine years of age. I was afraid of the end of the world, of circumstances in my personal life and in my family's life, and of world conditions present and future. There was never a moment's peace in my life as I worried about my own and my children's security in this world and in eternity. When I was twenty-eight years old, a lady, then a couple came to my home and wanted to do a Bible study. They went into great detail about the coming of Christ and the end of the world. They offered no hope. I was more terrified. I found out later that they were cultists."

(Next Jennie shares 2. *How she received Christ.*)

"My children attended Vacation Bible School at a small church in our neighborhood. Someone from the church came to my home and invited me to attend. I began to attend Bible study and worship there. Then a couple came to my home and shared about Jesus with me. They told me that if I would turn from my sins and trust Jesus, He would forgive my sins and come into my life. I was ready! I did exactly that. I prayed and asked God to forgive my sins and told Him I was ready to trust His Son as my Savior and Lord. He did come into my life and brought joy and peace."

(Here Jennie answers 3. *How Jesus Christ makes her life meaningful.*)

"I must confess that fears still do well up into my heart, but now I bring them to Jesus and He gives me peace through His presence. My life is no longer dominated by the insecurity of an uncertain future. I am trusting Jesus Christ for all I need in this life and for my eternity with Him.

"Has this kind of experience happened to you?"

The following is an actual *recovery testimony*.

"My life seemed fairly normal until the early years of my marriage. I struggled with being afraid. It grew worse when the children arrived. I prayed, read self-help books, and talked to a counselor, but I could not shake it.

"Then I discovered hope and help in Jesus when I began going to a Bible study with several friends. It was the teacher who helped me by sharing a similar problem with fear and how Jesus helped her move through it. Now I have Christ in my life and He's taken away my fear too.

"I am so glad that I have a personal relationship with Jesus because He gives me peace. Oh, sure I still struggle, but I get stronger every day. Jesus helps me understand my fears and live above them."

We have looked in this chapter at four ways to share the Gospel and lead a person to Christ. In the Appendix of *People Sharing Jesus* are several other approaches. You may choose the approach that is most natural for you to use and most nearly fits the need of the person with whom you share Jesus.

Let me encourage you to master as many of these approaches as you can and make them your own. Use them to share Jesus in your own way with the people you meet at the point of their need. Remember, successful sharing is sharing Jesus in the power of the Holy Spirit and leaving the results to God.

Conclusion

Sharing Jesus—
A Life Pattern

Sharing Jesus can absolutely be the normal pattern of a Christian's life. When something exciting and life-changing happens, we naturally want to tell it, since we usually talk about the things that are important to us. For the divine, eternal Lord of Glory to come to live in our lives is the most important thing that can ever happen to us. The joy of salvation stimulates within us the desire to please Him and to share Him with others. We naturally want others to know Him too. You wouldn't have so diligently devoted yourself to studying this book if that natural desire wasn't true of you as well.

You and I want to make sharing Jesus the norm for our lives. It is the most exciting adventure in the world to join hands and hearts with Jesus as His disciples on a mission to share Him with others. Sharing Jesus is not an option. It is the commission of our Lord for which He has empowered us (Matt. 28:18–20). "But you will receive power when the Holy Spirit comes on you; and you will be my witnesses in Jerusalem, and in all Judea and Samaria, and to the ends of the earth" (Acts 1:8 NIV).

Jesus' strategy in Acts 1:8 for reaching our world comes down to bands of believers grouped together for ministry. He first gave His strategy to a local church in the first century—the church in Jerusalem. It can be summarized in two words: *Go tell.* Taking this commission seriously, the disciples shared Jesus, saturating Jerusalem with the Gospel until the Gospel witness overflowed through Judea, extended to Samaria, and spread to the ends of the earth.

The entire undertaking seemed impossible. The first-century believers were ordinary people, few in number, and with very limited resources. Yet they simply did what He said, and the good news about Jesus spread rapidly.

Sharing Jesus where we are, like those early Christians, is the place to start. When you think about it, where else *could* you witness? Where we are with the relationships and acquaintances we have is the place where God can begin to use us mightily. There are some Christians who feel that they would be the greatest witnesses in the world if they were just in Brazil, in Africa, or in some other foreign country. But they are not lifting their finger in an effort to share Christ with their neighbors, with people at work or school, or with their family and friends. There is something wrong with that!

The strategy has not changed! It is still every Christian's assignment to share Jesus with others. Along with the assignment, God made it possible for us to accomplish it. He would never send us out to do the impossible. He has given us the equipment to share Jesus consistently. God has empowered us by giving us all we need to share Jesus.

First, God has *given us a changed life through the indwelling presence* of Christ. The Christ-centered, Spirit-filled, abundant life is characterized by the fruit of the Spirit. The fruit that influences people toward Christ includes "love, joy, peace, patience, kindness, goodness, faithfulness, gentleness and self-control" (Gal. 5:22 NIV). As we live the life of continuing unbroken fellowship with the Father, unbelieving people are impacted by this quality of life. They often become open to our witness. They are interested in what we say because they have seen how we live. We must *live the life.*

Second, God has *given us the power to be mighty witnesses through the indwelling presence of the Holy Spirit.* We must be available to Him to share Jesus as He gives us *divine appointments.* The Holy Spirit gives divine appointments to each of us frequently. It happens when our path crosses the path of someone who needs Christ. We have the opportunity to seek to share Jesus with the person as the Holy Spirit directs. The Holy Spirit helps us verbally give the Gospel to people in such a way that they can understand and respond to the claims of Christ on their lives, so both the life we live plus the words we speak equal our story to share Jesus.

Both a changed life and verbal witness on the part of Jim and Flo resulted in reaching Frank and Nancy, their next-door neighbors in the air force base housing community, for Christ. The two couples had perpetual conflict. Flo and Nancy, both hot-tempered, were archenemies. They quarreled almost daily about their children, who played together. It appeared that both of these couples would be unlikely possibilities to be reached for Christ. But they were reached showing the power of the team of three—the Word of God, the work of the Holy Spirit, and the witness of the believer to Christ. Because you are one of that team of three, God can use you too to reach the lost for Christ.

Jim and Flo became acquainted with Christians on the base. Through hearing the Word of God, they became convicted of their need for the Savior. A concerned Christian sensed their spiritual need and shared Jesus with them. Soon they trusted Jesus. Immediately their lives changed, and they began to demonstrate the fruit of the Spirit. The change was quickly evident to Frank and Nancy.

Jim and Flo went to a church near the base. They began to grow and share Christ with their friends. Several friends came to Christ and went with them to their church. They began to participate in Bible study, worship, and activities designed to reach the lost for Christ.

It was not long until Flo realized that she had a responsibility to God not only for her friends but also for her enemy next door. Through prayer, she found strength to apologize to Nancy, asking her forgiveness. Nancy was overwhelmed! She could not believe what had happened and told her husband, "Anything that can make that kind of difference in Flo, I've got to check out! This is amazing!"

The next Sunday Frank and Nancy were present at the worship services of Jim and Flo's church. A couple of nights later, Chris followed up in their home. Frank sat across from Chris on the sofa with a can of beer in one hand and a cigarette in the other. As he blew smoke, he said, "I believe in Christ, but I can't be a Christian! I'm a master sergeant in the air force, but I have a part-time job where I am paid well. There are some things I am doing that I don't think I can give up to be a Christian."

Chris determined to be sensitive to Frank's need and share in a noncondemning and nonthreatening way. "Frank," he said, "I did not come to talk to you about what you are or are not going to give up. I came to talk to you about Jesus. When you receive Him into your life, He'll guide you in what to do and what not to do."

Frank seemed to be relieved. He had anticipated being condemned or reprimanded for his behavior. He shared freely as Chris guided the conversation using **FIRM**. They discussed Frank's family and background in West Virginia. They talked about his interests in airplanes and world travel. Frank talked openly about religion and the lack of meaningful religious experience in his life.

Then Chris took the opportunity to share the message with him. "Frank, may we take your Bible and read about a man whose heart was so empty that he came to Jesus in the middle of the night to find the answer to life's greatest questions?"

"Sure," Frank responded as he took the huge family Bible from the shelf in the living room.

They turned to John 3. Chris led him in a dialogue through John 3:1–18 in much the same way it is presented in Chapter 11 of this book. When they finished reading and discussing, Chris asked if they could have prayer. Frank was glad to do so. Chris did not ask him to trust Christ at that time, even though he was open. He decided to leave him to the convicting work of the Holy Spirit.

The next Sunday night, Frank and Nancy were in church. When the invitation for people to receive Christ and confess Him was extended, the couple responded immediately. Frank was not asked what he would do about the problem areas in his life. Chris, Jim, Flo, and others at the church simply trusted God to lead Frank in his life for Christ.

And it happened! Two days later, early in the morning before work, Frank called and asked if he could meet Chris in his office immediately. He said he had to settle something *now!*

In the office, he asked, "Chris, I have a part-time job I believe is wrong for me to do. I can't do the things the job requires and have integrity and witness as a Christian. I told them that if I ever quit, I'd give two weeks' notice. What do you think I should do?"

Realizing he could not make Frank's decision for him, Chris said, "Frank, as Christians, we must be people who will keep our word. You're going to have to pray and let the Lord lead you."

After they prayed together, Frank went to the place of his part-time job, turned in his resignation, and told them why. He did give the two weeks' notice. But he never had to go back! Just before he was due back to work at the job, his unit was transferred to a distant area on temporary duty. The unit returned *in two weeks*.

Frank's life was transformed. He began to read his Bible at every opportunity. He took it to work with him to read when he finished his duties or on break. Airmen and civilians who worked with him would gather around and let him share his discoveries from the Bible. One after another, the people with whom he worked came to Christ too. The interest of the people around them multiplied as Jim and Flo continued to share Jesus with others and Nancy as well as Frank became people sharing Jesus.

Remember! God uses His Word, the work of the Spirit, and the witness of the believer to bring the lost to salvation. It is an unbeatable team! God used an unnamed Christian in the air force to reach Jim and Flo, He used Jim, Flo, and Chris to reach Frank and Nancy, and though they had been enemies, they became friends in Christ. Although they were new Christians, Frank and Nancy immediately led numbers of their friends to Christ. And God will use you too.

You will have the opportunity to be used by God to reach someone for Christ. And I know that, like me, the desire of your heart is to be sensitive to seek to share the Word of God with anyone with whom you come into contact. Our desire is to yield to the Holy Spirit to allow Him to use us in leading people to Christ.

God has a mighty army that can reach our world for Christ. It is the army of Christians armed with the Word of God and led and empowered by the Holy Spirit to be *People Sharing Jesus*.

Appendix

People need the Lord, and it is your desire and mine to help them in any way we can to come to know Him and experience His forgiveness and peace. People from all types of backgrounds, cultures, lifestyles, and philosophies need Him. We want to meet them where they are and share the message of Christ in such a way that they can respond to Him with understanding.

It is liberating to know that we are on that mighty team of three—the Word of God, the powerful Holy Spirit, and the Believer—that is empowered to successfully share Jesus and lead people to Him. The Scripture claims for itself that the "gospel of Christ is the power of God for salvation" (Rom. 1:16). This powerful Gospel needs to be shared with lost people at the point of their need.

In Chapter 11 and in this Appendix are several effective, natural, easy-to-master approaches for sharing Jesus. The different approaches will be helpful in equipping you to share Jesus in a person-centered way rather than using the same approach with everyone. You will find that some of the approaches are just to fit your own personality and giftedness as you share. Knowing how to use these and other approaches will enable you to share Jesus with the same person numerous times without saying exactly the same thing each time. This is often necessary for an effective witness in a continuing relationship.

The approaches are intentionally varied to teach you how

to use a booklet, you own testimony, and dialogue sharing. One of the key purposes is to show you how to use Bible passages interactively to lead a person to Christ. Those included in the Appendix are:

How to Share Jesus with a Child
How to Share the Message of the Cross
How to Share the Roman Road
How to Share Jesus with a Person Who Does Not
   Believe in God
How to Use "Life's Great Questions" to Share Jesus

How to Share Jesus with a Child

The door of opportunity to reach children for Christ is wide open. God's Spirit often speaks to the hearts of children and draws them to Christ. Childhood is when their hearts are tender and sensitive to the impressions of the Spirit of God. "Remember your Creator in the days of your youth, / before the days of trouble come and the years approach when you will say, / 'I find no pleasure in them'" (Eccl. 12:1 NIV).

In the Old Testament, Samuel heard the voice of God and mistook it for the call of the old priest, Eli (1 Sam. 3:4–11). Eli tenderly instructed him to answer, "Speak, LORD, for Your servant hears" (v. 9 NKJV). As in the case of Samuel, God speaks to the hearts of children today.

When Jesus' disciples refused to allow the children to come to Him, He reprimanded them, saying, "Let the little children come to Me, and do not forbid them; for of such is the kingdom of God" (Luke 18:16 NKJV).

Jesus' command is our authority and commission for reaching children. If we are obedient to Him, we will nurture, cultivate, and lead them to Him. Many of our greatest Christian leaders came to Christ as children.

A visit with children in their homes in the presence of their parents offers a prime opportunity to witness to entire families. Follow-up should be done with a child who has expressed an interest in following Christ during vacation Bible school, backyard Bible clubs, and other children's activities.

Great care must be exercised in sharing Jesus with children, however. Manipulation should never be used in leading a child to make a profession of faith in Christ. Sensitivity to the child's understanding and level of spiritual development is paramount. Care should be taken to make sure that the child's response is not an attempt to please the person witnessing.

The Concept

Children need to be encouraged, taught, and led to express their faith in Jesus from their own hearts. Do not put words in their mouths by asking leading questions. Ask open-ended questions rather than those eliciting yes or no answers. Guide them in conversation to express their own understanding and give their own responses.

If a child has not come to the point of understanding, conviction, and readiness to receive Christ, utilize the witness opportunity to teach him or her about Christ and salvation. Your sharing can be part of the process of growth in understanding that can ultimately result in his or her salvation.

The Conditions

Two conditions are necessary for salvation:

- Repentance from sin—that is, being conscious of

and convicted of sin, and willingness to turn from sin to God (John 16:8–11; Acts 20:21). A sign of readiness for salvation in a child is an understanding of and genuine sorrow for sin.

- Faith in our Lord Jesus Christ—that is, acceptance of Jesus as Savior and commitment to Him as Lord (John 3:16; John 1:12; Rom. 10:9–13).

The Conversation

Begin by putting the child at ease. Involve him or her in open, friendly, nonthreatening conversation about school, favorite subjects, favorite sports, etc.

Ask if you may discuss some questions. Tell the child that you would like to know what he or she thinks about these questions. Explain that there are no right or wrong answers.

(The purpose of these questions is to help determine the child's level of understanding and conviction of sin.)

- **Questions about Jesus:** "Tell me some of the things you know about Jesus. Who is He? What are some of the things He did?"

  Possible responses: "Jesus healed people. He helped blind people to see. He died on the cross for our sins."

  Ask: "Whose Son is Jesus?" (If the child does not understand about Jesus, use this excellent opportunity to teach.)

- **Questions about sin:** "You said that Jesus died for our sins. Tell me, what do you think sin is? What are some of the sins people do?"

Possible responses: "Sin is the bad things people do. Some sins are disobeying parents, lying, stealing . . ." (Discuss with the child God's commandments about sin.)

Ask: "Tell me, who do you think has sinned against God?"

Possible response: "Everybody."

"You mean everybody in the world?"

"Yes, everybody in the world."

"What about everybody in this room? Have all of us sinned?"

"Yes, everybody in this room has sinned."

"What about you? Have you sinned against God?"

At this point, if the child is not conscious of sin, the answer may be: "Oh, no. I would never do that!" However, if there is consciousness and conviction of sin, the answer may be: "Yes, I have sinned against God!"

A lovely nine-year-old girl responded to the question tearfully: "Yes, I have sinned! I am *such a sinner!*"

One might think, *Surely, this precious child could not be such a sinner*. It should be realized that the sin of a child is just as grievous and burdensome to him or her as the sin of an adult is to the adult. The child needs the ministry of parents and caring adults in helping to resolve the burden of guilt through the forgiveness of our Lord.

Ask: "How does it make you feel that you have sinned against God?"

Possible response: "Very bad!"

"God loves you very much, but He hates sin. God wants you to feel that way about your sin. He wants you to feel so badly about your sin that you ask God to forgive you and receive Jesus into your life. He will help you overcome sin."

(If the child says that he or she has not sinned, realize that this is an honest expression. Conviction for sin by the Holy Spirit has not yet been experienced. Use this time to teach the child about sin. Give assurance that the Holy Spirit will help him or her understand these things in time.)

> **Ask:** "Did you know that that's why Christ died on the cross—to pay for all of your sin?" (A good approach is to use the "Lifeline Illustration" to explain the Gospel. A child will understand the illustration.)

> **Ask:** "Would you like to pray and receive Jesus now? It will be a joy to me to pray with you and your parents as you call on Jesus and ask Him to forgive your sins and come into your heart."

(If the child is not ready, utilize this opportunity to teach him or her. Assure the child that the time will come when the Holy Spirit will prepare his or her heart to receive Christ. You may say, "I'm so glad you are concerned about spiritual things and interested in following Jesus.")

- **Involve the parents:** If they are Christians, ask them to pray for their child before he or she prays to receive Christ. If they are not Christians, after the child prays, ask them if they would like to pray, give thanks to God for saving their child, and receive Christ into their own hearts.

- **Follow up:** Explain to the child the meaning of confessing Christ publicly. Explain about following Christ in baptism. Teach the child how to grow as a Christian. Give the child and parents follow-up material. Ask the parents to study the material with their child. Make an appointment to come back a week later to share in study with them. Encourage them to become a part of a Bible class. Enroll them if possible.

How to Share the Message of the Cross

The story of the cross is captivating and convicting. Non-Christians may be turned off by organized religion and by invitations to church, but they will usually listen with interest to the biblical stories about Jesus. The cross is of particular interest. The message of the cross is the power of God to save. "For the message of the cross is foolishness to those who are perishing, but to us who are being saved it is the power of God" (1 Cor. 1:18 NIV).

The message of the shedding of the blood of Jesus for sin will often pierce hearts like nothing else can. Hearing about His loving and willing sacrifice stirs a person's mind, emotions, and will.

Because you have experienced the sacrificial love and forgiveness of our Lord, you are the perfect spokesman to take His message to others. No person in the world should be deprived of knowing what Jesus did on the cross. *Every* Christian should be committed to getting the message of the cross and the resurrection to *every* person.

The message of the cross can be easily memorized and the story told in your own words. Even hardened, hostile people have seen their resistance melt away as the story of the cross was told simply by a Christian.

If you will memorize seven events and some of the details surrounding them, you will be able to adequately summarize the "greatest story ever told." These seven events enable us to follow the footsteps of Jesus from the Garden of Gethsemane to the open tomb. The seven key events listed in chronological order are:

SHARING THE MESSAGE OF THE CROSS

STEP	SCRIPTURE	SETTING	PEOPLE PRESENT	KEY THOUGHT	RELATED DETAILS
①	Luke 22:40–50	Garden of Gethsemane	Jesus and Apostles Judas and Soldiers	Arrested	Jesus prayed Apostles slept Jesus agonized Jesus submitted Judas bretrayed
②	Matthew 26:57–68	Before High Priest and Sanhedrin	Jesus, High Priest, Part of Sanhedrin, Apostles at a distance	Tried	Jesus was struck with fists, spat upon, and mocked
③	Luke 23:1–6	Before Pilate	Jesus, Pilate, Priests, Sanhedrin, Crowd	Examined	Accused Jesus Examined Jesus Found no fault Sent Jesus to Herod
④	Luke 23:7–12	Before Herod	Jesus, Herod, Priests, Soldiers, Crowd	Mocked	Accused, Mocked Jesus Dressed Jesus in Herod's old royal robe Sent back to Pilate Herod and Pilate became friends
⑤	Luke 23:13–23	Before Pilate a second time	Jesus, Pilate, Soldiers, Priests, Crowd, Pilate's Wife	Sentenced	Barabbas released Crowd incited Crucifixion demanded Jesus scourged Pilate's wife warned Pilate washed his hands Pilate yielded to pressure Jesus sentenced to be crucified
⑥	Matthew 27:38–60 Luke 2332–56	Calvary	Jesus, Two thieves, Soldiers, Priests, Crowd, Disciples	Crucified	Nails driven through hands and feet Priests and crowd mocked Jesus' seven last words Darkness covered earth Jesus died Earth quaked Jesus was buried
⑦	Luke 24:1–12	Garden Tomb	Angels, Disciples	Raised	Jesus arose Jesus appeared Jesus ascended

1. Jesus Arrested in the Garden of Gethsemane (Luke 22:40–50).

2. Jesus Tried before the High Priest (Matt. 26:57–68).

3. Jesus Examined before Pilate the First Time (Luke 23:1–6).

4. Jesus Mocked before Herod (Luke 23:7–12).

5. Jesus Scourged by Pilate and Delivered to the Crowd (Matt. 27:11–31; Luke 23:13–23).

6. Jesus Crucified on Calvary (Matt. 27:33–60; Luke 23:32–56).

7. Jesus Resurrected from the Dead (Luke 24:1–12).

In sharing the message of the cross, begin with each of the seven steps and summarize the main thoughts in your own words. The following is an example:

Jesus Arrested in the Garden of Gethsemane (Luke 22:40–50)

On the night before He was crucified, Jesus withdrew with His disciples to a private place of prayer. There He agonized in prayer as He accepted on Himself the sins of the world. "Father, if you are willing," He prayed, "take this cup from me; yet not my will, but yours be done" (v. 42 NIV). As He continued to pray, so intense was His agony that He sweat great drops of blood. This is the blood shed for our sins without which there can be no forgiveness. "And according to the law almost all things are purified with blood;

and without shedding of blood there is no remission" (Heb. 9:22 NKJV).

The temple soldiers led by Judas came and arrested Jesus and took Him from the Garden to the court of the high priest. He would be tried in an illegal trial in the middle of the night. His disciples forsook Him and fled.

Jesus Tried before the High Priest (Matthew 26:57–68)

The high priest and the council interrogated and condemned Him. "But Jesus remained silent. The high priest said to him, . . . 'Tell us if you are the Christ, the Son of God.' 'Yes, it is as you say,' Jesus replied. 'But I say to all of you: In the future you will see the Son of Man sitting at the right hand of the Mighty One and coming on the clouds of heaven'" (vv. 63–64 NIV).

The high priest went into a rage and tore His robe. Then the Sanhedrin charged Jesus with blasphemy and illegally sentenced Him to death. "They spit in his face and struck him with their fists. Others slapped him and said, 'Prophesy to us, Christ. Who hit you?'" (vv. 67–68).

Since the Sanhedrin had no authority to order the death sentence, they took Jesus to Pilate, the Roman governor, to appeal for execution.

Jesus Examined before Pilate the First Time (Luke 23:1–6)

Jesus was accused of being an insurrectionist, refusing to pay taxes to Caesar, and claiming to be a king. But upon examining Him, Pilate declared that he found no fault in Him. Still, Pilate was afraid to let Jesus go because the crowd was demanding His crucifixion, accusing Him of stirring up the people from Galilee to Jerusalem. When Pilate heard that Jesus was from Galilee, he conceived of a way out of his dilemma. He would send Jesus to Herod, the ruler of Galilee, who was in Jerusalem for the feast.

Jesus Mocked before Herod (Luke 23:7–12)

Herod was greatly pleased to see Jesus, hoping to see Him perform some miracle. Herod asked Him many questions, but Jesus did not answer. The chief priests and scribes vehemently accused Jesus, after which Herod and the soldiers ridiculed and mocked Him, then dressed Him in one of Herod's old royal robes and sent Him back to Pilate. As a result, Herod and Pilate, who had been enemies, became friends.

Jesus Scourged by Pilate (Matthew 27:11–31; Luke 23:13–23)

Pilate further examined Jesus, while the religious leaders continued to demand His death. Then Pilate conceived the idea of releasing a prisoner to show mercy in recognition of the feast of the Passover, thus hoping to be able to free Jesus. He selected the notable criminal and insurrectionist, Barabbas, to give the crowd a choice.

"'Which of the two do you want me to release to you?' asked the governor. 'Barabbas,' they answered. 'What shall I do, then, with Jesus who is called Christ?' Pilate asked." Again the crowd, incited by the religious leaders, shouted, "Crucify Him!" (Matt. 27:21–23 NIV).

At that point Pilate's wife appeared, asking her husband to have nothing to do with this just man. She said that she had had a terrible dream about Him. Pilate took a basin of water and washed his hands saying, "I am innocent of the blood of this just Person. You see to it" (v. 24 NKJV).

Pilate ordered the soldiers to strip Jesus of His clothing and beat him with a cat-of-nine-tails whip, tipped with bone, metal, and lead balls. Many men died under the severity of this kind of scourging. Often, the victim's eyes were knocked out, rib bones were bared, and the stomach ripped open. The blood of Jesus ran down to the pavement—the blood without which there is no forgiveness for sin.

They crowned Him with a crown of thorns and beat it down into the flesh of His head with a reed. The blood flowed out and matted His face and beard—the blood without which there is no remission for sin. They put on Him a scarlet robe, placed a reed in His hand, and mocked Him, saying, "Hail, King of the Jews!" (v. 29).

Then Pilate delivered Jesus to the crowd. They placed the beam of the cross on His back and led Him away to be crucified. Exhausted from all that had transpired, Jesus stumbled under the weight of the cross. At that point, they hailed a passerby, Simon of Cyrene, and made him bear the cross. Making their way up the Via Dolorosa to Golgotha, the hill of the skull, they crucified Jesus where common criminals were executed.

Jesus Crucified on Calvary (Matthew 27:33–60; Luke 23:32–56)

The soldiers threw Jesus to the ground and stretched out His arms on the beam of the cross. One of them pounded spikes through the palms of His hands, then through His feet, fastening Him to the cross. They lifted up the cross and, with a thud, dropped it into the hole, tearing Jesus' soft flesh. "And sitting down they watched him there" (Matt. 27:36 KJV). Like uncivilized savages, these doctors of law and philosophy—religious and political leaders—watched with sadistic glee, even joining the crowd in mocking Him. "If You are the Son of God, come down from the cross!" Then again, "He saved others; Himself He cannot save. If He be the King of Israel, let Him now come down from the cross, and we will believe Him" (Matt. 27:40, 42 NKJV).

Looking down from the cross, His voice breaking with pathos and agony, Jesus cried, "Father, forgive them; for they know not what they do" (Luke 23:34 KJV). The words of that prayer ring down through the ages and reach all the way to you and me. Thank God that He shed His blood for us!

The sun refused to shine on that hideous scene on Calvary. From about nine o'clock in the morning, darkness covered the land. Suddenly at about noon, Jesus' horrifying cry pierced the darkness, "'Eli, Eli, lama sabachthani?' that is, 'My God, my God, why have you forsaken me?'" (Matt. 27:46 NKJV).

At that moment God did a miracle. He reached out into all of time to bring together all the sin of all humanity and concentrate all of our guilt into the body of Jesus. On the cross the One who knew no sin became sin for us (2 Cor. 5:21). Jesus, who had never sinned, suddenly felt the combined intensity of all the guilt of all sin of all time. God, who cannot look upon sin, withdrew from His own Son. For the first time in all eternity, the Son was separated from the Father. Our sin killed Him!

Just before He died, Jesus cried out, "It is finished" (John 19:30). This was not the defeated cry of a man facing the dismal end. It was a shout of triumph! He had accomplished that for which He had come into the world. The sin debt was paid in full. He had provided the way for humankind to come to God. And with the words, "Father, into Your hands I commit My spirit" (Luke 23:46 NKJV), Jesus released His spirit to the Father.

After Jesus died, they pierced His side with a spear. Out flowed blood and water. Blood and water in that area of His body indicates that His heart had ruptured. So intense was His spiritual agony that it broke His heart.[†]

At the cross, Joseph of Arimathea and Nicodemus, who had been secret disciples, received courage for open confession of their commitment. They came forward to ask for the body of Jesus. They took His body down from the cross and prepared it for burial, and afterwards laid it in the tomb of Joseph.

Jesus Resurrected from the Dead (Luke 24:1–12)

On the third day after Jesus' death, some of the women came to the tomb to find the stone rolled away and His body missing. Jesus appeared to His disciples at least eleven times following His resurrection. "By many infallible proofs He showed Himself alive from the dead" (Acts 1:3). He gave instructions and commands. He promised to send the Holy Spirit to enable His followers to take the good news of His death, burial, and resurrection to every person in their world. Then He ascended to take His place at the right hand of the Father to guarantee access to God through Him (Acts 1:1–11).

Now, by faith, you, too, can turn from your sins and receive forgiveness for all your sins and be born into the family of God. Like Joseph and Nicodemus, you will have the courage and joy to openly confess Him as your Savior and Lord.

May I ask you now to pray with me? Ask Jesus, who died to pay for your sins and rose again, to forgive your sins and to come into your heart.

How to Share the Roman Road

The book of Romans contains an orderly presentation of the power of the Gospel. It presents the need of sinful humanity, the remedy for sin, and the way to receive salvation. The following passages have been called "the Roman Road to Salvation":

- Romans 3:23

- Romans 6:23

- Romans 5:8

- Romans 10:9–13

Believer: "May I share with you from the Bible how you can come to Christ and receive the gift of salvation? The book of Romans clearly points the way."

Seeker: "Yes, you may."

Believer: "Romans 3:23 is a summary of chapters 1–3. It tells about the condition of every person before God. Please read the verse aloud." (Reading the verse aloud utilizes the senses of sight, speech, and hearing to impress the Scripture more strongly on the mind of the seeker.) "What does this verse mean to you?"

Seeker: "It means that everyone has sinned."

Believer: "What about you yourself? Have you sinned against God?"

Seeker: "Yes, I know I've sinned too."

Believer: "I could not point my finger at you and condemn you as a sinner. I'm a sinner too. Notice that verse 22 says that there is no difference. We have all sinned. We are all in the same boat, and it is a sinking ship. We have all fallen short of what God has for us. The word picture is that of an archer shooting an arrow. It falls short and misses the target. This is what sin is. It is missing the target or mark that God has set for our lives.

"Romans 6:23 tells us the result, or 'wages,' of sin. If a person works all week, he expects to be paid. According to this verse, what is the payment—wages—of sin?"

Seeker: "It says that the wages of sin is death."

Believer: "Yes. The payment for sin is death. This death is speaking of eternal death or separation from God. Thank God, the verse does not stop there! He inserted the word *but*. And what an important word it is. It says that the gift of God is eternal life through Jesus Christ, our Lord. You can't buy, merit, nor earn it. The question is 'How do you get a gift?'"

Seeker: "You have to accept a gift."

Believer: "You're right! Jesus is God's gift to us. Through Him we have eternal life. Please read Romans 5:8 aloud and see why God gave His Son for us."

Seeker: (Reads Romans 5:8.) "God gave His Son because He loves us."

Believer: "Now let's look at Romans 10:9 and 13. It tells us how to come to God and receive His forgiveness and deliverance. These verses indicate three action verbs we are to do. 'That if you confess with your mouth, "Jesus is Lord," and believe in your heart that God raised Him from the dead, you will be saved . . . for, "Everyone who calls on the name of the Lord will be saved."' What are the three things we are to do?"

Seeker: "Confess Jesus is Lord, believe God raised Him from the dead, and call on Him."

Believer: "May I ask you, do you believe He is God's Son and that He died for you, that God raised Him from the dead, and that Jesus is Lord?"

Seeker: "Yes I do."

Believer: "Then will you call on Him, express your faith to Him, and ask Him to forgive your sins? It will be a joy for me to pray with you and for you. It is not the words of the prayer that make the difference but the attitude and faith of the heart that God responds to. But this is the kind of prayer, if you can pray and mean it from your heart, God will answer: *Dear Lord, I do believe that You are God's Son. I believe You died for me and rose from the dead. I know that I have* sinned and fallen short of what You have planned for me. Please forgive me. Come into my heart and help me to be the person You want me to be. Thank You for hearing my prayer and coming into my life. Amen.

Seeker: Yes, I do want to ask Him to come into my life.

- If the seeker is not ready to trust Christ and call on Him, you may have prayer for them and ask again if the seeker will trust Christ or discuss with them what seems to be standing in the way.

- If the seeker prays, then follow the suggestions in Chapter 10, Step 5. Pray with the seeker to express joy and thankfulness to the Father for His blessing of revelation.

How to Share Jesus with a Person Who Does Not Believe in God

A person who declares that there is no God or states that he or she does not believe in God is one who desperately needs someone to care and share Jesus and to spend enough time to help them work through the barriers they have. This person in all probability does not know what the Bible says about God and salvation. The purpose of this presentation is not to be a full and exhaustive plan for dealing with a person who does not believe in God. Instead, it is designed to help begin the dialogue, plant the seed of God's Word, and help move the person to a higher level of spiritual understanding and openness to the Gospel.

It is imperative that unbelievers have the opportunity to hear and/or read the powerful Word of God and experience the enlightening work of the Holy Spirit. Remember, God uses three things to bring the lost to Him: the Word of

God, the work of the Holy Spirit, and the witness of the believer. Of course, through the power of the Gospel and the mighty work of the Spirit, the person may become open to receive Christ immediately, like William, about whom I will share with you later.

Most atheists do not have a genuine intellectual problem with the existence of God. Their problem is usually moral and spiritual, coming from a life that is inconsistent with God's nature and Word. They want to run their own lives the way they see fit and the existence of God crowds that out. Others, having experienced disappointment in life, may have become bitter. In either case, they justify themselves in their own minds by relegating God to a place of nonexistence. They cannot stand to have their lives exposed to the light of the life-changing Gospel. Often they are at the ignorance or hostility level of spiritual understanding. They need someone who will love them, share the Gospel with them, and leave the results to the Holy Spirit.

To initiate a sharing opportunity, you may ask: "Have you thought about what the statement 'There is no God' really says? It assumes that the person making the statement knows everything! We know that is not true. If there is even one fact that is not known or one place they have not been, there remains the possibility that there is a God and the person just does not know Him."

You may go on to note that physical evidence supports the existence of God:

1. *The evidence of Creation points to God.* The vast complexity of the universe demands that there be a creator. The improbable number of cause-and-effect events it would take to create a universe leads us to God as Creator.

2. *The existence of order in the universe points to God.* The universe is governed by universal principles such as mathematical laws, chemical laws, and natural laws. If

you were to jump off the roof of your house, you would not fall *up*; you would fall *down*. As many times as you jump, if you are able to do it more than once, you will fall down! The law of gravity is a reality. It is consistent. An orderly universe gives evidence of an orderer. The existence of a plan presupposes that there is a planner. The Bible teaches that God is the Orderer and Planner of Creation.

3. *The creation of life points to God.* There is no life without a lifegiver. The Creator is God. God created humans in His image. Thus, humanity is capable of living in communion with Him. God has communicated His purpose to us.

Moving into a discussion of the purpose of God for humanity may find resistance. The person may respond by saying that he or she does not believe in the Bible. If so, you can usually receive the person's permission to share from the perspective of the biblical point of view. It is important that the person understands what the Bible teaches about Creation, the purpose of human life, and salvation to build faith. Remember, "Faith comes by hearing, and hearing by the Word of God" (Rom. 10:17 NKJV).

If there is resistance to the biblical account, you may gain permission to discuss it by asking, "You have indicated that you do not believe the Bible. Let's not discuss whether or not you believe it at this point. Rather, may we discuss what it teaches about our origin, purpose, and destiny in life? May I share with you what I understand it says about these basic issues of life?"

A scenario that illustrates this point occurred one night in Atlantic City, New Jersey. While Scott was sharing Jesus with some people on the beach, he encountered an angry young man named William. As Scott began to share with him, William objected, "I don't believe that. I don't believe the Bible!"

"That's okay, William," Scott replied gently. "I'm not asking you to *believe* the Bible. I'm asking you *to be informed* about what it teaches." After Scott had shared for a while longer and had gone through a witnessing booklet with him, he asked, "William, I want to ask you if you will believe in Jesus and trust Him now as your Savior?"

To Scott's surprise, William's response was immediate. "Yes, I will!"

Right there on the beach, William bowed with Scott and prayed, trusting Christ as His own Savior and Lord.

4. After you have discussed 1, 2, and 3, use the Lifeline Illustration in Chapter 11 or an evangelistic booklet.

5. Proceed as far as the person will permit following the Steps in Chapter 10.

Leave the door open for future times of sharing if he or she does not receive Christ. Reaching the unbeliever will involve time and sensitivity in the witnessing relationship as the Holy Spirit works. Pray daily for him or her. Trust the Holy Spirit to continue to do His work in the person's heart and mind.

How to Use "Life's Great Questions" to Share Jesus

Some of the people with whom you will have an opportunity to share Jesus will be defensive if the subject of God or the Bible is initially approached. They do, however, have intense feelings and questions about the great questions of life. You may find it very helpful to dialogue about some of them. In the course of the dialogue, you may use the conversation guide **FIRM** in Chapter 4.

F — Family
I — Interests
R — Religion
M— Message

As you move into the discussion of religion or religious background, you may use the "Great Questions" approach. (The following is based on a dialogic witnessing approach developed and written by Dr. Ken Hemphill, author and seminary president.)

Ask, "What are the 'big questions' for which you are seeking answers?" (Dialogue about the person's questions. One or all of the following questions will usually surface. As you dialogue, write down the one word that summarizes the question. Do not attempt to answer the questions until you have written the word for each of them.)

1. **Origin:** "Where did I come from? Did I just happen or was I an intentional creation?"

2. **Purpose:** "Why am I here? What am I here for?"

3. **Values:** "How should I live today? What is right and wrong?" Many are frustrated by the complexities of life. For them, the rules they were taught as children no longer seem to apply.

4. **Destiny:** "Where am I going after death?"

Origin: "Where Did I Come From?"

Start with **origin.** You may say, "The answer to this question will determine the way we answer the other questions on the list. There are two possible answers to the question of origin. First, that all intelligent life came through chance mutation. Nothing plus infinite time plus chance equals everything. That option has never been totally convincing to me, but what other options do we have?

"There is really only one other option. Behind it all there exists an intelligent creative Being or Force who started the process and has continued to guide it with some ultimate purpose in mind." (You will notice that the name for God has not been used nor has any process of creation been mentioned. At this point, we are simply laying the foundation. Give the person with whom you are sharing opportunity to respond.)

Purpose: "Why Am I Here?"

After you have agreed on this basic truth, you are ready to move to a second but related question—our **purpose** for existing. You may say, "If we can agree that a creator exists, then you are a created being. The purpose for any created being or thing can only be determined by the creator who designed the creation."

The person may ask, "How do I know that purpose?" (If the question is not asked, you may surface it.)

Share from your own experience. "If you like, I can tell you how I know and what that purpose is for my life." (Give an opportunity for response.) "I find my answer for the purpose question in the Bible. I was created in the image of my Creator so I could know Him in personal intimacy. He created me so that I could live in relationship with other persons and to exercise good stewardship over all the rest of creation."

Values: "How Should I Live?"

Continue the discussion by saying, "Now, we are ready to answer the question about **values**. There are three possible answers to this question. One, we could allow each person to determine his or her own values and laws." (Give an opportunity for response.)

"The second option is that we could have a popular vote and determine the law by a simple majority rule. There is a down side to this system of determining laws. To illustrate, passengers on an airplane could take a vote that it would be best for everyone to throw another passenger out of the plane. But, of course, this decision would violate the rights of the person thrown out of the plane." (Give opportunity for response.)

"The third option is that the Creator designed a world in which certain physical laws, such as the law of gravity would govern the world, and certain moral and spiritual laws would govern our relationships within that world. If God created an orderly physical world, does it not make sense to you that He would ensure that there was also moral order?" (Give opportunity for response.)

"Here again I find these laws and values in the Bible. The Ten Commandments cover all the basic areas of our two fundamental relationships—our relationship with God and with our fellowman. These very commandments are the foundation for the legal system of our country. God Himself is the only one who has the right or ability to determine how we should live."

Destiny: "Where Am I Going after I Die?"

You may continue to dialogue by saying, "This leaves us with one more question: "Where are you going?" This is one of the most critical questions that we will ever answer because all of us will one day face death. There are three possible answers.

"One, life is all there is and when we die, we return to dust and cease to exist.

"Two is the circular view of history where everything that exists is part of the oneness of the universe which is itself eternal. You may be reborn in several different lifetimes or even life forms.

"Perhaps, if your are good, you will be born into a higher or more glorious body. But what if you're not?" (Give time for response.)

"The evidence we see around us indicates that people do evil things. If we also take into account the bad thoughts and motives as well as the good things we fail to do, we might realistically look at ourselves. But let's assume the best: that you advance to the next level when you die. Once you have reached your final stage of human existence, what then? The end result of successive positive reincarnations is said to be this blissful union with the one, the divine force, which is described as 'nirvana,' a mindless and person-less existence. This idea is not far from dying, returning to dust, and ceasing to exist.

"There is a third alternative. It is the natural conclusion to all we have talked about. You were created in the image of God so that you might know Him and serve His purpose now and for all eternity. Your Creator is eternal by His very nature and thus He alone can give eternal life. He has made you so that you can live eternally with Him. Would you like to know how you can do that?"

At this point, if the response is positive, you may share a Gospel presentation, using a witnessing booklet, the *People Sharing Jesus* New Testament outline, the Lifeline Illustration, or another meaningful approach.

Several methods of sharing the plan of salvation have been presented in this chapter. It will be a strength to your personal witness to be able to share the Gospel in a variety of ways, depending upon the particular need of the unbeliever.

As you continue to share Jesus faithfully, the Holy Spirit will lead you to develop ways to share that are natural to you. He will use your own personality and unique gifted-ness for His glory. As Christians obediently share Jesus with the people they know and meet, our communities will be sown with the seed of the Gospel, and multitudes will come to know and follow Him.

† Dr. William Barclay writes, "It may well be true that Jesus died literally of a broken heart. Normally, of course, the body of a dead man will not bleed. It is suggested that what happened was that Jesus' experiences—physical and emotional—were so terrible that His heart was ruptured. When that happened, the blood of the heart mingled with the fluid of the pericardium which surrounds the heart. The spear of the soldier pierced the pericardium and the min-gled fluid and blood came forth. It would be a poignant thing to believe that Jesus died, in the literal sense, of a broken heart" (William Barclay, *The Gospel of John, vol. 2* [The Westminister Press, Philadelphia, 1956] 304.)